The Super Simple Programming Book

Learn Basic Programming Concepts With Python

Dr. Edwin R. Torres

ISBN: 9781718198456

DEDICATION

I dedicate this book to Wendy, Nicole, Ashley, and Max. You are the most important people in my life. I love you.

CONTENTS

ACKNOWLEDGMENTS

I would like to thank my colleagues Steve Foote and Brendan Smith for providing feedback on this book and continuing to support my career pursuits. I really appreciate their help and encouragement.

PREFACE

You *can* learn programming. You really can. There is nothing mysterious about it. There is nothing to fear. *Anyone* with a brain can become a programmer. If you like to solve problems or create things, then you will *love* programming. This book will not make you an expert programmer, but it will start you on the right path to becoming one. You will not learn every detail about programming; there are other books for that. Instead, you will learn essential programming concepts through simple Python programs. These fundamental concepts appear in most programming languages, so it is important to learn them. This book will help you learn any programming language.

This book is a super simple approach to programming. You can do this. Enjoy the ride!

1 HELLO WORLD!

Before we start, there are a few things to go over. This first chapter describes how to download, install, and use Python, the programming language you will learn and use. By the end of this chapter, you will know how to create, save, and execute a simple Python program. This is an important chapter, because you will create Python programs in every chapter of this book. But first…

Why Python?

Python is a great programming language to learn. Here are some reasons why:

1. *Python is free.* It costs you nothing to download and use it.
2. *Python is simple.* Python statements are simple to read, understand, and use, even for new programmers. Python is simple enough for beginners, yet advanced enough for experienced programmers.
3. *Python is available on most platforms.* Python is available on the major computing platforms such as Windows, Mac, and Linux.
4. *Python has an extensive standard library.* Python comes with lots of built-in functions, procedures, and properties for common programming tasks.
5. *Python is extensible.* You can create your own Python library modules and access the many existing third-party modules.
6. *Python is popular.* According to the 2018 Stack Overflow Developer Survey, Python is one of the most popular and fastest-growing programming languages today.

Get Python

Before getting Python, check if you already have it. Start a Command Prompt (Windows computer) or Terminal (Mac or Linux computer) and type: `python -V`. If the Python version appears, then your computer already has Python. If not, you must download and install it.

Which Version?

Python 2 and Python 3 are the two current versions of Python. Python 2 is scheduled to retire in 2020, so learning Python 3 is preferable. However, Python 2 typically comes with Mac and Linux computers today. To make it easier to get started with Python, the programming examples in this book work with *both* Python 2 and Python 3. However, there is one exception: Python 3 examples use `input()` to read string input, while the Python 2 examples use `raw_input()` to read string input. A later chapter will emphasize this exception.

Download and Install Python

From your web browser, go to Python.org and download the Python installer file for your operating system. Run the installer file to install Python. This will install the Python programming language, a helpful integrated development environment called IDLE, and some help files. Now that you have Python, it is time to try it out.

Python From the Terminal

You can run Python programs directly from the terminal. The first step is to create and save your Python program in a text file with the `.py` extension. Use any plain text editor on your computer to create the Python text file. There are many available text editors. On Windows computers, there are *Notepad* and *WordPad*. On Mac computers, there is *TextEdit*. On Linux computers there are *nano*, *vi*, and *emacs*. Save the following one-line Python program to a text file named `hello.py`:

```
print("Hello World!")
```

Next, open a terminal window and go to the folder where the `hello.py` text file is. Finally, use the `python` command to run the program:

```
$ python hello.py
Hello World!
```

In the output above, the `$` character is the command prompt of this terminal window (your command prompt may vary). After the command prompt, type **python hello.py** and press **Enter**. This executes the program and displays the **Hello World!** output message in the terminal window. Congratulations! You just wrote your first Python program!

This is one way to create and execute a Python program, and it works well for the practice exercises in this book. But there is another, more graphical way to create and execute Python programs.

Python From IDLE

You can run Python programs from the IDLE environment. From your computer, find and execute the Python IDLE program. IDLE is a lightweight development environment for creating, editing, debugging, and executing Python programs. It is more powerful than a plain text editor. Starting IDLE opens the Python Shell, a window where you can execute Python statements directly. In the Python Shell, type the following statement and press enter:

```
>>> print("Hello World!")
Hello World!
```

In the above output, the `>>>` characters are the command prompt for the Python Shell. Type `print("Hello World!")` after the command prompt. Finally, press `Enter` to execute the command and display the `Hello World!` output message in the Python Shell. You can try out different Python statements using this approach.

The Python Shell also lets you create and save a Python program to a text file. This is a good approach for the programs in this book. Here are the steps to create a Python program, save it as a text file, and execute it in IDLE:

1. Start IDLE.
2. From the Shell menu bar at the top, select `File > New File`. This will open a blank text editor window.
3. In the text editor window, type this program:

   ```
   print("Hello World!")
   ```

4. From the editor menu bar, select `File > Save As...`, pick a folder location, type `hello.py` as the file name, and click the `Save` button. This will create a text file called `hello.py` in the folder you selected.
5. From the editor menu bar, select `Run > Run Module` to run the Python program. This will execute the Python program, bring the Shell to the foreground, and display the program output.

Practice this approach for creating and executing Python programs. You will do this often in the following chapters.

Programming Basics

Python executes programs line-by-line. Here is a Python program that prints three messages to the console:

```
# Print three messages
print("Hello Nicole!")
print("Hello Ashley!") # second message
print("Hello Max!")
```

Python executes these statements in sequential order. First, it prints the message `Hello Nicole!` Next, it prints the message `Hello Ashley!` Finally, it prints the message `Hello Max!` The first line of this program, starting with the `#` symbol, is a comment. Comments are for documentation purposes only. Python ignores all comments in your programs. All characters to the right of the `#` symbol are the comment. Line 3 shows a comment that follows a Python statement on the same line. Although Python ignores all comments, comments provide useful explanations for anyone who reads your programs.

Beware of typos in your programs. Just one typo will cause your entire program to fail. Look at this program:

```
print("I like the movie Elf.)
```

If you run this program, you will immediately see an error. This is an example of a *syntax* error. The problem is with the string value: `I like the movie Elf.`. The string starts with a double quote character, but it is missing the double quote character at the end of the string. All string values must be enclosed by double quote characters. Here is the corrected program:

```
print("I like the movie Elf.")
```

This program properly terminates the string with the second double quote character.

Be careful with indenting in Python programs. Python requires you to indent code blocks. Here is an example:

```
if (1 < 2):
print("1 is less than 2")
```

This program has a syntax error. Line 2 must be indented, since it is part of the `if` statement above it. Use spaces to indent Line 2 and be consistent while indenting different statements. Also remember to indent for different levels (i.e., nested statements). Here is the corrected program:

```
if (1 < 2):
  print("1 is less than 2")
```

These are just some of the concepts to keep in mind while working through this book. The following chapters will describe programming statements in more detail.

Final Tips

Make sure you can comfortably create and execute a simple Python program (like you did earlier in this chapter). You will do this a lot in the following chapters. This is an important activity, because it allows you to practice programming on your own. That is how you will become an expert.

In the following chapters, the programming examples show syntax highlighting and line numbers. The line numbers are for reference only. Do not type the line numbers when trying out the programs on your own. Here is an example of a formatted code snippet:

```
1  print("Practice")
2  print("makes")
3  print("perfect.")
```

In the code listing above, the line numbers precede each programming statement. When trying out this program, do not type the line numbers (i.e., `1`, `2`, or `3`). Otherwise, you will experience syntax errors. The console output of programming examples will appear like below:

```
Practice
makes
perfect.
```

Work through this book in sequential order. Some chapters assume that you already read previous chapters. The early chapters are building blocks for the later ones.

If you have any troubles with Python, *do not panic.* There are plenty of helpful resources. The Python website (Python.org) has programming documentation and guides. Another excellent resource is Stack Overflow (Stackoverflow.com). This is a free online community that lets you post specific programming questions and receive quick, helpful answers. Users rank answers based on correctness, clarity, and brevity. You will find that most of your programming questions already have answers on Stack Overflow. For example, Google this text: *python specify new line stack overflow*. Find the first Stack Overflow result and click it. Explore the question and answer to learn how to print a new line in Python.

Try not to get overwhelmed by the many programming statements and concepts. Remember that computers only do *four* things: input, processing, output, and storage. Keep this in mind as you learn programming. You do not have to learn everything about programming now; you can learn new concepts later, when you need them. This book will teach you basic, fundamental, programming concepts, and you will be able to explore these concepts during your own practice sessions. I strongly recommend that you do this.

You can do this. Programming is not just for computer geniuses. If you can cook from a recipe, drive a car, or follow instructions, you can program a computer. All it takes is logical thinking, patience, and practice. It does not matter if you were a straight-A student or if you barely graduated. Programming is a skill that anyone can learn with reading and practice. By the end of this book, you will be surprised by how much programming you learned. And it will only be the beginning of your journey. This book will equip you to learn more about Python or any programming language you choose.

Finally, you can contact me. I am on Twitter @realEdwinTorres . My email address is edwintorres@gwu.edu. Please send me your comments, questions, and suggestions. This is the first edition of this book. If you find errors or have suggestions, please let me know. I will acknowledge you in the next edition. Thanks in advance for your help!

Lastly, have fun! Programming is fun! Trust me.

2 DATA

Computers need data to process. They process data to make information. Without data, computers would be useless. Data are all around us, and they take different forms. Programs use data in operations and expressions. This chapter describes how to represent different types of data in your programs.

Data Types

Data represent things in the real world. Five common types of data in programming are integer, float, Boolean, character, and string. There are other data types, but these are the more common ones. Before describing these data types, we must first discuss variables.

Variables

A *variable* is a name of some location in memory that can hold data. For example, here is a variable that holds a string value:

```
greeting = "Hello"
```

In this short program, the variable is `greeting`, and the value is the string `"Hello"`. The = operator assigns the string data to the variable. When the program executes, the computer stores the string `"Hello"` in some location in memory. To access that string, use the variable `greeting`. You could have named the variable something else, like `x` or `s1`. But the name `greeting` is more descriptive, and it makes your program more readable. Variables are useful, because you can use them in the same way that you use data. Here is a previous program from Chapter 1 that uses a variable:

```
greeting = "Hello"
```

```
2   print(greeting + " Nicole!")
3   print(greeting + " Ashley!")
4   print(greeting + " Max!")
```

Line 1 of the program stores the string **"Hello"** in the variable **greeting**. Line 2 combines the value of the **greeting** variable with the string **" Nicole!"** to form the new string **"Hello Nicole!"**. It uses the **+** operator to combine the two string values into a new string. Finally, the **print()** statement prints the new string value. Lines 3-4 perform similar operations.

Variables make your programs more maintainable. For example, if you want the previous program to output **Hi** (instead of **Hello**) to each student, you only have to change Line 1:

```
1   greeting = "Hi"
2   print(greeting + " Nicole!")
3   print(greeting + " Ashley!")
4   print(greeting + " Max!")
```

Assigning a new string value to the **greeting** variable conveniently changes the three lines of program output. Even this simple example shows the power of variables. Variables can hold different types of data. Here is an example that uses numeric data:

```
1   x = 5
2   y = 10
3   z = 6
4
5   avg = (x + y + z) / 3
6
7   print(avg)
```

Lines 1-3 declare three variables and assign three numbers to them. Line 5 performs a mathematical calculation to determine the average and assigns the result to the **avg** variable. Line 7 prints the **avg** variable.

There are a few rules to follow when naming variables in Python. First, variable names must start with either a letter or the '_' character. Second, the rest of the variable name may include letters, numbers, or the '_' character. Third, variable names are case sensitive. In other words, the variables **myvar** and **myVar** are two different variables. Finally, variable names may not be reserved words. In other words, you may not use the name **for** as a variable, because for is the loop statement in Python. Here are some examples of good and bad variable names in Python:

```
1  # good variable names
2  total = 9
3  First_Name = "Edwin"
4  temp1 = 98.7
5  _username = "etorres"

6  # bad variable names
7  2wheeler = "Bicycle" # cannot start with a number
8  print = True # print is a reserved word
9  $dollars = 100 # cannot start with a $ sign
10 my$var = 1.1 # cannot use $
```

Lines 2-5 declare legal variable names. Lines 7-10 declare illegal variable names, and each line causes a syntax error. The comment on each line explains why the variable is illegal.

Variables let you store and access different types of data. The remaining sections use variables with some common data types in programming.

Integer

The *integer* data type represents numbers that do *not* have decimal places. Integers may be positive, zero, or negative. Use integers to represent numbers like ages or quantities. Programs may use integer values in mathematical calculations. Here is a program that uses integers to represent the elevations relative to sea level for some U.S. locations:

```
1  Coachella_elev = -72 # 72 feet below sea level
2  New_Orleans_elev = -7
3  Denali_elev = 20320 # 20320 feet above sea level
4  Tenleytown_elev = 410
```

Note how the variable names above use the '_' character to increase readability. Line 1 declares a variable named Coachella_elev and assigns it the value -72. To indicate that an integer is negative, precede it with the - symbol. It is not necessary to precede positive numbers with a + symbol, since it is implied. The integer value on Line 3 is positive 20320.

A program may print integers, just like strings. Here is a program that uses integers to store and print the quantities of three fruits:

```
1   num_apples = 10
2   num_pears = 15
3   num_cherries = 0
4
5   print( str(num_apples) + " apples")
6   print( str(num_pears) + " pears")
7   print( str(num_cherries) + " cherries")
```

Here is the output of the program:

```
10 apples
15 pears
0 cherries
```

Lines 1-3 declare three variables and assign three integer values to them. Before combining an integer value with a string value, the program must first convert the integer to a string. Lines 5 uses the `str()` function to convert the integer value `10` in `num_apples` to the string `"10"`. Next, the program uses the `+` operator to combine the string `"10"` with the string `" apples"` to create the new string `"10 apples"`. Finally, Line 5 uses the `print()` statement to print the new string to the console. Lines 6-7 perform similar operations. If you only want to print the variable itself, you do not have to use the `str()` function. The `print()` function can print a variable directly:

```
1   num_apples = 10
2   num_pears = 15
3   num_cherries = 0
4
5   print( num_apples )
6   print( num_pears )
7   print( num_cherries )
```

Here is the output:

```
10
15
0
```

Lines 5-7 use the `print()` statement to simply print each variable. An integer variable may hold any integer value, as well as any expression, function, or operation that returns an integer value. Here is an example:

```
1  import math
2
3  total = 0
4  f = math.factorial(3)
5  x = (9 * 2) + 2
6
7  print(total)
8  print(f)
9  print(x)
```

Line 1 of this program imports the `math` library; a later chapter discusses how to use libraries. Line 3 declares a variable named `total` and assigns the value `0` to it. Line 4 declares a variable named `f` and assigns the return value of a function to it. The `math.factorial(3)` function calls the `factorial()` function from the `math` library. It passes in the parameter `3` to compute `3!`. The return value is `6` (i.e., `3 * 2 * 1`). Finally, the program assigns `6` to the variable `f`. Line 5 declares a variable named `x`. The mathematical equation on Line 5 evaluates to `20`, and the program assigns `20` to the variable `x`. Lines 7-9 print the values of the three variables. Here is the program output:

```
0
6
20
```

Float

The *float* data type represents numbers that have decimal places. These numbers may be positive or negative. Use the float data type to represent decimal numbers like weights or temperatures. Programs may use float values in mathematical calculations. Here is a program that stores and prints temperature readings for three planets:

```
fahr_venus = 875.5 # Venus temp. in Fahrenheit
fahr_mars = -25.8
fahr_pluto = -387.2

print("Venus temperature: " + str(fahr_venus))
print("Mars temperature: " + str(fahr_mars))
print("Pluto temperature: " + str(fahr_pluto))
```

Lines 1-3 declare three variables and assign three float values to them. Once again, it is necessary to use the `str()` function to convert a float value to a string value before combining it with another string to create a new string. Lines 5-7 print the variables with descriptive strings. Here is the output:

```
Venus temperature: 875.5
Mars temperature: -25.8
Pluto temperature: -387.2
```

Here is a program that stores and prints *pi*:

```
pi = 3.14159265359

print("pi is: " + str(pi))
```

This program shows that a float value may have several decimal places.

Boolean

The Boolean data type represents data that may be either true or false. A Boolean variable in Python may only hold either the literal value `True` or the literal value `False`. Use Boolean variables to represent true/false, yes/no, or on/off values. Here is a program that uses two Boolean variables:

```
1   switch_on = False
2   store_open = True
3
4   print("Light switch on? " + str(switch_on))
5   print("Store open? " + str(store_open))
```

Here is the output of the program:

```
Light switch on? False
Store open? True
```

The `switch_on` variable on Line 1 contains the literal value `False`. It represents a switch that is currently off. The `store_open` variable on Line 2 contains the literal value `True`. It indicates that the store is open. It is necessary to use the `str()` function to convert a Boolean value to a string value before combining it with another string. Boolean values have another purpose in programming; they provide the conditions for selection statements. A later chapter discusses selection statements.

Character

The *character* data type represents a single letter, digit, symbol, or whitespace. A character is surrounded by single quotes. A character can represent most symbols that you can type on a keyboard, like the `'!'`, `'1'`, or `'*'` characters. It may be printable or non-printable. Here is an example:

```
1   grade = 'A'
2   exclamation = '!'
3   tab = '\t'
4   space = ' '
5   one = '1'
6
7   print("My grade: " + grade)
8   print("Hi" + exclamation)
9   print("Hello" + tab + "world!")
10  print("chicken" + space + "nuggets")
11  print("Place: " + one)
```

Here is the output:

```
My grade: A
Hi!
Hello	world!
chicken nuggets
Place: 1
```

Line 1 of this program declares a variable named **grade** and assigns the `'A'` character to it. A character must be surrounded by single quotes (`''`). Line 2 declares a variable named **exclamation** and assigns the `'!'` character to it. The tab character on Line 3 is unprintable, but you do see a tabbed space between **Hello** and **world!** in the third line of the output. The tab character requires an *escape sequence* when you use it. In other words, you must precede the **t** character with a backslash (\) symbol to distinguish a tab from the lowercase `'t'` character. Here is an example that shows this difference:

```
plain_t = 't'
print(plain_t)

tab = '\t'
print(tab + "Hello")
```

In the above program, Line 1 assigns the plain character `'t'` to the variable `plain_t`. Line 2 prints the `plain_t` variable to the console. Line 4 assigns the tab character `'\t'` to the variable `tab`. Line 5 prints the `tab` variable, along with the string `"Hello"` to the console, which effectively indents the output. Here is the output:

```
t
        Hello
```

The tab character creates the spacing before the `"Hello"` string above. You cannot see the actual tab character, but you can see the spacing it creates when you print something immediately after it.

You must also escape the double quote character, since Python uses it to surround a string. Here is an example:

```
print("\"To be or not to be.\"")
```

The first and last double quote characters indicate the start and end of the string. The two pairs of \" characters inside the string represent the actual double quote character ("). Here is the output:

```
"To be or not to be."
```

Since the backslash (`'\'`) character is used for an escape sequence, you must escape it if you want to print the actual backslash character. To print the actual backslash character to the console, escape it with a backslash:

```
1   backslash = '\\'
2
3   print(backslash) # prints \
```

Line 1 of this program uses an escape sequence to indicate the literal backslash character. Line 3 prints the backslash character to the console. Here is the output:

```
\
```

Another non-printable character is the newline (`'\n'`) character. The newline character is just like any other character (e.g., `'a'` or `'%'`). However, the newline character is special. There is no visible output, except that it forces the console output to the next line. You must use an escape sequence to distinguish the newline character (`'\n'`) from the actual `'n'` character. Here is an example:

```
1   newline = '\n'
2   #
3   print("Red" + newline + "Red" + newline + "Wine")
```

Here is the output:

```
Red
Red
Wine
```

Line 1 of this program assigns the newline character ('\n') to the `newline` variable. This character is escaped with a backslash character. Line 3 combines three string values with the newline characters to form a new string. Printing the new string one character at a time yields the output above. The `print()` statement on Line 3 prints each character of the string. When it reaches a newline character, the program forces output to the next line.

One final note is that characters are more like strings than numbers. You may combine characters to form a string. Here is an example:

```
1   str = '1' + '2' + '3'
2   print(str)
3
4   ans = 1 + 2 + 3
5   print(ans)
```

Line 1 of this program combines three characters to form the string `"123"`. Line 2 prints the string, and `123` appears in the console. Line 4 *adds* the integers `1`, `2`, and `3` and stores the result in the `ans` variable. Line 5 prints the `ans` variable, which outputs `6`.

String

The *string* data type represents a sequence of characters. Use double quote characters to specify a string. String data may represent text, alphanumeric, or symbol information. Here is an example:

```
str1 = "abcd1234_+$%&^"
str2 = "3\t2\t1"

print(str1)
print(str2)
```

Here is the output:

```
abcd1234_+$%&^
3       2       1
```

Line 1 declares a string variable named **str1** and assigns it the string **"abcd1234_+$%&^"**. The string is surrounded by double quotes, and it includes these 14 individual characters: **abcd1234_+$%&^**. The string on Line 2 includes five characters: **'3'**, **'\t'**, **'2'**, **'\t'**, and **'1'**.

In Python, the string data type is a *class*. Unlike primitive data types like integer and character, the string class provides useful and convenient string methods. Here is a program that creates three string variables, assigns the name of a university to each variable, prints a leading sentence, and prints the variables:

```
university1 = "University of Maryland"
university2 = "University of Delaware"
university3 = "Johns Hopkins University"

print("Three excellent universities are:")
print(university1)
print(university2)
print(university3)
```

Here is the output:

```
Three excellent universities are:
University of Maryland
University of Delaware
Johns Hopkins University
```

You have already seen string values in previous programs. But a string is a class, so it has useful, built-in methods. Here is a similar program that demonstrates the **len()**, **upper()**, and **lower()** string functions:

```
university1 = "University of Maryland"
length1 = len(university1)
upper1 = university1.upper()
lower1 = university1.lower()

print("Length is: " + str(length1))
```

```
7   print(upper1)
8   print(lower1)
9   print(university1)
```

Here is the output:

```
Length is: 22
UNIVERSITY OF MARYLAND
university of maryland
University of Maryland
```

The `len()` function on Line 2 accepts the `university1` variable as an argument and returns the length of the string that the variable references. The string `"University of Maryland"` has 22 characters (including the spaces), so the function returns `22`. The program assigns `22` to the `length1` variable. The string class provides the `upper()` function to return an uppercase version of a string. To call this function, append it to a string variable (or value) with a dot (`.`) symbol. Line 3 uses the `upper()` function to return a new string that is an uppercase version of the string value in the `university1` variable. The `lower()` function on Line 4 works the same way, but it returns a lowercase version of the string. It is important to note that the value in the `university1` variable remains unchanged throughout the program. The `upper()` and `lower()` functions return a new copy of a string value and leave the original string value in the `university1` variable unchanged.

Here is a program that demonstrates the `strip()` string method:

```
1   name = "  Wendy  "
2   print("{" + name + "}")
3
4   name = name.strip()
5   print("{" + name + "}")
```

Here is the output:

```
{  Wendy  }
{Wendy}
```

The `name` variable contains the string `"  Wendy  "`, which has two spaces before and after the name. The `strip()` function on Line 4 returns a new version of the string that removes any leading or trailing whitespace (i.e., space or tab characters). The function does not change the original variable `name`. But since the program assigns the stripped string back to `name` on Line 4, it effectively changes it to a new value. There are many more methods in the string class. You do not have to learn them all now. Learn them when you need to.

Summary

Programs need data to process. Without data, programs would be a lot less useful. In the real world, data take different forms. Programs have data types to represent this real world data. Program variables let programs store and reference data. Now that you understand data and variables, the next step is to learn how to perform operations on data. Variables and data are the operands. Special symbols in Python are the operators.

3 OPERATORS

Operators are special characters in a programming language that operate on data. Some operators require two data values (i.e., operands), and some require one. There are operators that assign values to variables, compare values, perform calculations, and perform operations. The following paragraphs describe some popular operators in programming.

Assignment Operator

The assignment operator (=) assigns a value to a variable. The value may be data or a variable. You have seen this operator in previous programs. Use assignment whenever the program needs to store or change values. This program uses the assignment operator to assign values to three variables:

```
age = 21
weight = 178.6
occupation = "student"
```

Here is a program that assigns a variable to another variable:

```
name1 = "Wendy"
name2 = name1

print(name1)
print(name2)

name1 = "Ed"
```

```
 8
 9  print(name1)
10  print(name2)
```

Line 1 of this program assigns the string value `"Wendy"` to the variable `name1`. Line 2 assigns the contents of the variable `name1` to the variable `name2`. Note that `name1` and `name2` each have their own copy of the `"Wendy"` string value. Lines 4-5 print the values of the `name1` and `name2` variables:

```
Wendy
Wendy
```

Line 7 changes the value of the `name1` variable to `"Ed"`. This does not affect the value of the `name2` variable. Here is the output of Lines 9-10:

```
Ed
Wendy
```

Here is a program that uses the assignment operator (=) to change the value of the `age` variable three times:

```
1  age = 21
2  age = 22
3  age = 23
4  print(age)
```

Line 1 of this program assigns `21` to `age`. Line 2 assigns `22` to `age`; this replaces the previous value of `21`. Line 3 assigns `23` to `age`. Finally, the last line prints the current value of the `age` variable: `23`.

The assignment operation assigns raw data, the result of an expression, the result of a function, or the result of some other operation to a variable. The examples in the next sections illustrate this.

Arithmetic Operators

Arithmetic operators perform mathematical calculations on data. These operators are like the arithmetic operators you learned in elementary school. Here is a program calculates the result of `2.0 + 2.0`:

```
result = 2.0 + 2.0
print(result) # prints 4.0
```

Line 1 in this program shows that the addition operator (+) in programming is just like the addition operator in mathematics. Note that when the addition operator (+) is used with string data, it combines the operands to form a single string. Here is a program that demonstrates other arithmetic operators:

```
1   a = 3.0
2   b = 2.0
3
4   result = a + b
5   print(result) # 5.0
6
7   result = a * b
8   print(result) # 6.0
9
10  result = a - b
11  print(result) # 1.0
12
13  result = a / b
14  print(result) # 1.5
15
16  result = a ** b
17  print(result) # 9.0
```

Lines 1-2 of this program declare and initialize variables a and b. The operation on Line 16 is an example of exponentiation (**). It raises a to the power of b (i.e., a^b).

Just like in mathematics, the order of operations matters. Do you remember the *Please Excuse My Dear Aunt Sally* rule from elementary school? It means that arithmetic operations execute in this priority order: parentheses, exponentiation, multiplication, division, addition, and subtraction. Python programs follow this priority order. Here is a program that demonstrates this operator precedence:

```
a = 3.0
b = 2.0
c = 4.0

result = a + b * c  # do b * c first
```

```
6   print(result) # 11.0
7
8   result = (a + b) * c  # do a + b first
9   print(result) # 20.0
10
11  result = a ** b - c  # do a ** b first
12  print(result) # 5.0
13
14  result = a + c / b - 1.0  # do c / b first
15  print(result) # 4.0
```

Lines 1-3 of this program declare and initialize three variables. Line 5 demonstrates that you must perform the multiplication (i.e., `b * c`) first. Line 8 shows how parentheses change the priority order. In this case, the parentheses make the `a + b` operation the first priority. Line 11 shows that exponentiation must occur first. Line 14 shows that division must occur first.

Python has a `math` library that provides built-in math functions. Here is a program that demonstrates some of these `math` functions:

```
1  import math
2
3  x = math.pow(2.0,3.0) # 8.0
4  x = math.sqrt(9.0) # 3.0
5  x = math.pi # 3.14159265359
```

Line 1 of this program imports the `math` module, so you can use these built-in `math` functions. Line 3 calls the `pow()` function to raise `2.0` to the power `3.0`. The program assigns the result to the variable `x`. Line 4 calls the `sqrt()` function to take the square root of `9.0`. The program assigns the result to the variable `x`. Line 5 assigns the constant `math.pi` to `x`. There are many more `math` functions that you can explore on your own.

Integer Division

The examples in the previous section use float values in the arithmetic operations. Arithmetic operations with integer values work the same way, except for division. In integer division, division with two integer values yields an *integer* result. To specify integer division, use the integer division operator (//). Here is an example:

```
a = 9
b = 2
```

```
3
4 result = a // b # integer division
5 print(result) # 4
```

We know that 9 divided by 2 is 4.5, but the above program prints 4. Line 4 uses the integer division operator (`//`) to perform integer division. The integer `2` divides `9` evenly `4` times, with a remainder of `1`. Integer division returns the integer divisor (i.e., `4`) only. To retrieve the remainder of integer division, use the modulo operator (`%`):

```
1 a = 9
2 b = 2
3
4 result = a % b
5 print(result) # 1
```

Using two integer values with the modulo operator yields an integer result. In Line 4 of the above program, the integer `1` is the remainder when you divide the integer `9` by the integer `2`.

One useful function of the modulo operator is to determine if a number is odd or even. Simply divide the number by `2` and check the remainder. If the remainder is `0`, then the number is even. If the remainder is `1`, then the number is odd. Here is an example:

```
a = 11
b = 10

remainder = a % 2
print(remainder) # 1; so it is odd

remainder = b % 2
print(remainder) # 0; so it is even
```

Mixing Integer and Float

If you mix integer and float values in the same arithmetic operation, the integer value is *widened* to a float value. Thus, the operation becomes a float operation, and the result is a float value. Here is an example:

```
a = 9
b = 2.0
```

```
print(a + b) # 11.0
print(a - b) #  7.0
print(a * b) # 18.0
print(a / b) #  4.5
print(a % b) #  1.0
```

Unary Operators

Unary operators are operators that operate on a single value. The + and - unary operators are like the positive and negative symbols in mathematics. You may omit the + operator for positive numbers, because it is implied. Here is an example:

```
1  a = -3
2  b = +2
3  print(a) # -3
4  print(b) # 2
5
6  a = -a
7  b = -b
8  print(a) # 3
9  print(b) # -2
```

Line 1 of this program assigns the value `-3` to the variable `a`. Line 2 assigns the value `+2` to the variable `b`. Lines 3-4 print the values of `a` and `b`. Line 6 applies the `-` operator to the variable `a`. This effectively flips the sign, changing `-3` to `3`. Line 7 performs the same operation, changing `+2` to `-2`.

Another unary operator is the *negation operator* (`not`). This operator changes a `True` value to `False` and a `False` value to `True`. Here is an example:

```
1  e = True
2  print(e) # True
3  print(not e) # False
4  print(e) # True
```

Note that the value of `e` never changes, since the only assignment occurs on Line 1 of the program. Line 2 prints the current value of `e`. Line 3 prints the result of negating `e`, but it does not change `e`. Line 4 prints `e` to show that it is still `True`.

Comparison Operators

Comparison operators compare two values and return a Boolean (`True` or `False`) result. These operators are like their mathematical counterparts. The comparison operators are: equal to (==), not equal to (!=), greater than (>), less than (<), greater than or equal to (>=), and less than or equal to (<=). It is important to note the difference between the assignment operator (=) and equality operator (==). Do not confuse the two. Here is a program that demonstrates the comparison operators with integer values:

```
1   a = 3
2   b = 2
3   c = 3
4   print(a == 3) # True
5   print(a == b) # False
6   print(a == c) # True
7   print(2 == 2) # True
8   print(a != b) # True
9   print(a != c) # False
10  print(a > b)  # True
11  print(a < b)  # False
12  print(a >= b) # True
13  print(a <= b) # False
14  print(a >= c) # True
15  print(a <= c) # True
```

Lines 1-3 assign integer values to three variables. Line 4 performs the comparison `a == 3` to check for equality. Since `a` currently holds the value `3`, then this comparison is `True`. Line 5 performs a similar comparison between variables `a` and `b`. Lines 6-15 perform other comparisons, and the comments show the results of those comparisons.

Since comparison operators return a Boolean value, you may assign a comparison to a variable. Here is an example:

```
1   a = -2
2   negative = a < 0
3   print(negative) # True
```

Line 1 of this program assigns the value `-2` to the variable `a`. Line 2 tests to see if `a` is less than `0`. Since `a` is `-2`, then the comparison returns `True`, and the program assigns `True` to the `negative` variable.

Comparison operators compare other data types too. Here is a program that compares Boolean, character, string, and float data:

```
1   isOpen = True
2   response = 'Y'
3   color = "red"
4   temp = 98.7
5   print(isOpen == True)    # True
6   print(isOpen != False)   # True
7   print(isOpen != True)    # False
8   print(response == 'N')   # False
9   print(response != 'N')   # True
10  print(response == 'Y')   # True
11  print(color == "red")    # True
12  print(color == "green")  # False
13  print(color != "green")  # True
14  print(temp == 98.7)      # True
15  print(temp > 100.3)      # False
16  print(temp <= 98.7)      # True
```

Lines 1-4 declare four variables and assign values to them. The remaining lines perform comparisons with those variables and print the results. The comments after each statement are the results.

Conditional Operators

Conditional operators operate on two Boolean values. They compare the two Boolean values and return a Boolean result. The conditional operators are `and` and `or`. An `and` operation evaluates to `True` if *both* values are `True` and `False` otherwise. An `or` operation evaluates to `True` if *at least one* of the values is `True` and `False` otherwise. Here is a program that demonstrates the fundamental cases of the `and` and `or` operations:

```
print( True  and True )  # True
print( True  and False ) # False
print( False and True )  # False
print( False and False ) # False

print( True  or True )   # True
```

```
7   print( True  or False )  # True
8   print( False or True )   # True
9   print( False or False )  # False
```

Line 1 of this program uses the **and** operator to compare the **True** and **True** values. The result is **True**, and the **print()** statement prints **True**. The remaining statements of the program are similar, and their results follow the rules of the **and** and **or** operators.

Here is a program that uses the **and** operator to decide whether to wear a raincoat:

```
1   isCloudy = True
2   isHumid = True
3   wear_raincoat = isCloudy and isHumid # True
```

In this simple example, it must be *both* cloudy and humid to wear a raincoat. Since both variables on Lines 1-2 are **True**, the **and** operation on Line 3 evaluates to **True**, and the program assigns **True** to the **wear_raincoat** variable. Here is a program that uses the **or** operator to check if the variable **resp** is **'Y'** or **'y'**:

```
1   resp = 'y'
2   isValid = (resp == 'Y') or (resp == 'y') # True
```

This example checks if the variable **resp** is either **'Y'** or **'y'**. This is a common way to validate a user response, since it checks both uppercase and lowercase values of the letter Y. Line 2 of this program performs two comparison operations to compare the **resp** variable to **'Y'** and **'y'** respectively. The **or** operator compares the results of those two comparison operations. At least one of the comparisons must be **True** for the **or** operation to return **True**.

You may combine unary, comparison, and conditional operators to create more complicated Boolean expressions. See if you can predict the output of this sample program:

```
a = 3
b = 2
result = (a > b) and (b > 1)
print(result)

r = 0 # menu options: 0, 1, 2
```

```
result = (r == 0) or (r == 1) or (r == 2)
print(result)

# Teenager?
age = 13
result = not (age < 13 or age > 19)
print(result)
```

Summary

One of the primary functions of a program is to process data. Programs use special symbols called operators to operate on data and produce results. This chapter described some of the widely used operators in programming. Representing and processing data is vital. The advanced programming concepts in the following chapters build on these foundational concepts.

4 OUTPUT

Output is how a program presents information to users. It is one of the major functions of a computer. There are many types of output. This chapter describes two common forms of output in programming: console output and file output.

Console Output

Console output from a program goes to the program window. This may be the Python Shell or a terminal window. Many of the previous examples output to the console. This program prints the string `"Hello World!"` to the console:

```
1   print("Hello World!")
```

The `print()` statement on Line 1 accepts a string as a parameter and displays that string to the console. To print multiple lines of output, use multiple `print()` statements in your program:

```
print("Nicole")
print("Ashley")
print("Max")
```

Here is the console output:

```
Nicole
Ashley
Max
```

Each `print()` statement in the previous program prints its string and advances output to the next line. Here is a program that prints a triangle to the console:

```
1  print("   *")
2  print("  ***")
3  print(" *****")
4  print("*******")
```

Here is the output:

```
   *
  ***
 *****
*******
```

Lines 1-3 print strings that have spaces. The spaces do appear in the console output. Another way to print strings on multiple lines is to use the newline (`'\n'`) character. Here is a program that creates the same output as a previous program, but with a single `print()` statement:

```
print("Nicole\nAshley\nMax")
```

In the above program, the single string `"Nicole\nAshley\nMax"` includes two newline characters. The `print()` statement prints each character of the string to the console. When it encounters the newline character, it forces the console output to the next line. The result is three lines of output, like before:

```
Nicole
Ashley
Max
```

To create tabbed output, use the tab (`'\t'`) character. The tab character forces the console to the next tab stop. This makes it easy to print data in columns, for example:

```
print("10\t20")
print("30\t40")
print("50\t60")
```

Here is the output:

```
10      20
30      40
50      60
```

Since the tab character is just a character, you may include multiple tab characters in a string. This program creates multiple columns:

```
print("X\tO\tX")
print("O\tO\tX")
print("O\tX\tO")
```

Here is the output:

```
X       O       X
O       O       X
O       X       O
```

A program can output both data and variables. Use the addition operator (+) to combine string data and variables into a single string. Then print the string. Here is an example:

```
1   first_name = "Wendy"
2   students = 15
3   print(first_name + " teaches at a preschool.")
4   print("She has " + str(students) + " students.")
```

Here is the output:

```
Wendy teaches at a preschool.
She has 15 students.
```

Lines 1-2 declare two variables and assign values to them. Line 3 uses the + operator to combine the `first_name` variable with the string `" teaches at a preschool."` to form a new string. The `print()` statement on Line 3 prints the new string. Line 4 uses the `str()` function to convert the `students` variable to a string. The + operators combine the three string variables to form a new string. Finally, the `print()` statement on Line 4 prints the new string.

File Output

File output from a program goes to a file on the computer. The file remains on your computer after the program completes. Writing to a file is like writing to the console, except the program writes the output to a file on your computer. Here is a program that outputs to a text file:

```
1   f = open('output.txt', 'w')
2   f.write('Knights\n')
3   f.write('Blue Hens\n')
4   f.write('Terps\n')
5   f.close() # important!
```

Line 1 of this program calls the `open()` function to open a new text file named `output.txt` for output. The function creates this file in the same folder where you execute the program. The `'w'` parameter causes the program to create a new file or replace the file if it already exists. The `open()` function returns a file object, and the program assigns the object to the variable `f`. Lines 2-4 use the file object to call the `write()` function to write some strings to the file. These strings include the newline character at the end. Line 5 calls the `close()` function to close the file object. It is important to close the file object when you are done with it, because it releases the file resource to the computer. When the program terminates, the `output.txt` file contains this text (you can verify this by opening `output.txt` in a text editor):

```
Knights
Blue Hens
Terps
```

Just like with console output, the tab character creates columns in text files. Here is a program that writes fruit inventory data to a file:

```
1   f = open('output.txt', 'w')
2   f.write('Fruit Inventory\n')
3   f.write('---------------\n')
4   f.write('Date\tApples\tOranges\t Pears\n')
5   f.write('08/01\t 10000\t  20000\t 30000\n')
6   f.write('08/02\t 10002\t  20032\t 30022\n')
7   f.write('08/02\t 10010\t  20038\t 30019\n')
8   f.close() # important!
```

Lines 2-3 of this program write the table header to the output file. Line 4 writes the column headings, separated with the tab character and one space.

Lines 5-7 write the column data to the file, separating the column data with tab characters and spaces. This lines up the data with the column headings. Line 8 closes the file. Here are the contents of the **`output.txt`** text file:

```
Fruit Inventory
---------------
Date  Apples   Oranges  Pears
08/01 10000      20000  30000
08/02 10002      20032  30022
08/02 10010      20038  30019
```

The same data could be stored in a comma-separated values (CSV) file. Spreadsheet programs like Microsoft Excel can read these files. The file must have the extension `.csv`. Here is a program that creates a CSV file named `output.csv` with the fruit inventory data:

```
f = open('output.csv', 'w')
f.write('Date,Apples,Oranges,Pears\n')
f.write('08/01,10000,20000,30000\n')
f.write('08/02,10002,20032,30022\n')
f.write('08/02,10010,20038,30019\n')
f.close() # important!
```

Here are the contents of the file:

```
Date,Apples,Oranges,Pears
08/01,10000,20000,30000
08/02,10002,20032,30022
08/02,10010,20038,30019
```

The program omits the title in the CSV file. Only the column headers and data appear in the CSV file. If you open this file in Microsoft Excel, it will display the columns correctly.

To append to (not replace) an existing file, use the parameter `'a'` in the `open()` statement. For example, run this program *five* times:

```
f = open('output2.txt', 'a')
f.write(' Veritas vos liberabit.\n')
f.close()
```

Even though this program only writes one string to the **`output2.txt`** file, it will contain five lines. Each time you run this program, it adds another line to the file. Here are the contents of `output2.txt` after five executions:

```
Veritas vos liberabit.
Veritas vos liberabit.
Veritas vos liberabit.
Veritas vos liberabit.
Veritas vos liberabit.
```

Summary

Programs use output to present information to users. Two common types of program output are console output and file output. Console output is a visual display of characters on the console window. This output disappears when you close the console window. File output goes to a file on your computer. To view file output, open the file with a text editor or use a system command. For example, on a Linux or Mac terminal, you can type `cat output2.txt` to display the file contents on the console. The output file remains on the computer, even after the program completes. To remove the file, use a system command to delete it.

5 INPUT

Input is another major function of a computer. Program input is important, because it provides data for processing. A program may accept input from a variety of sources. This chapter describes program input from two common sources: the console and a file.

Console Input

Console input is input that a user enters in the console. This is usually in the form of key presses on a keyboard. Console input lets a user provide data to a program while it is executing. This makes programs more dynamic and useful.

String Input

Important Note: string input in Python 2 differs from string input in Python 3. If you are using Python 2, use the `raw_input()` function instead of the `input()` function in the string input examples below. If you are using Python 3, the string input examples will work as is.

To accept string input from the user, use the `input()` statement. Here is program that asks the user to enter a name and says `Hello` to that name:

```
your_name = input('What is your name? ')
print("Hello " + your_name + "!")
```

In this program, the `input()` function accepts a string parameter to prompt the user. It prints this string to the user before accepting input. After the user types a name and presses the `Enter` key, the program assigns the name to the **your_name** variable. Line 2 outputs a message with that name. Here is a sample run of the program:

```
What is your name?  Max
Hello Max!
```

Here is a program that accepts the name, address, and telephone number from a user and prints out the inputted values:

```
name = input('Name? ')
address = input('Address? ')
phone = input('Phone? ')

print('You entered:')
print(name)
print(address)
print(phone)
```

Here is a sample run of the program:

```
Name? Ed
Address? 1 Elm St.
Phone? nnn-nnn-nnnn
You entered:
Ed
1 Elm St.
nnn-nnn-nnnn
```

Numeric Input

To accept numeric input from the user, use the **input()** function. Here is a program that accepts a numeric grade as input and prints out that grade as a string:

```
grade = input('Enter grade: ')
print("Your grade is: " + str(grade))
```

Here is a sample run of the program:

```
Enter grade: 99.4
Your grade is: 99.4
```

Accepting console input makes programs more useful, because the user

supplies the data. Here is a program that asks the user to enter three numeric grades and displays the average of those grades:

```
 1  grade1 = input('Enter grade 1: ')
 2  grade2 = input('Enter grade 2: ')
 3  grade3 = input('Enter grade 3: ')
 4
 5  grade1 = float(grade1)
 6  grade2 = float(grade2)
 7  grade3 = float(grade3)
 8
 9  average = (grade1 + grade2 + grade3)/3.0
10
11  print("The average is: " + str(average) + ".")
```

Here is a sample run:

```
Enter grade 1: 99.2
Enter grade 2: 81.3
Enter grade 3: 76.4
The average is: 85.6333333333.
```

Lines 1-3 of this program accept three grades from the user. Lines 5-7 use the `float()` function to convert each grade from raw input to a floating-point number and store the result in a variable. Line 9 calculates the average of the three grades. Line 11 prints out the average.

File Input

File input comes from an existing file on the computer. The program opens the file, reads data from it, and closes the file when finished. The first step is to create a sample text file for input. You may use any text editor to create the text file. Windows has the *Notepad* text editor. Mac and Linux have text editors such as *nano* and *vi*. Use a text editor to create a file named `towns.txt` on your computer. Type the following text in the file:

```
Marlboro
Manalapan
Toms River
```

Save and close the file. In the same folder where you saved the `towns.txt` text file, create this program:

```
1   f = open('towns.txt', 'r')
2
3   line = f.readline()
4   line = line.rstrip()
5   print(line)
6
7   line = f.readline()
8   line = line.rstrip()
9   print(line)
10
11  line = f.readline()
12  line = line.rstrip()
13  print(line)
14
15  f.close()
```

The code to open a file for input is like the code to open a file for output. The above program will look for the `towns.txt` file in the same folder and open it for input. The primary difference is the mode parameter. The `'r'` parameter on Line 1 indicates that the program only reads from (not writes to) the file. Line 3 calls the `readline()` function to read a single line from the input file. Next, Line 3 stores the line in the `line` variable. Line 4 uses the `rstrip()` function to remove any trailing whitespace characters from the `line` variable; in this case, it removes the newline character at the end of the line. Then, Line 4 stores the result back in the `line` variable. Line 5 prints the `line` variable to the console. Lines 7-13 repeat the process to read the next two lines from the input file and print them. Line 15 calls the `close()` function to close the file. Here is the output of the program:

```
Marlboro
Manalapan
Toms River
```

Here is another example that reads temperatures from a text file and calculates the average temperature. First, create a text file named `temperatures.txt` with the following content:

```
80.4
100.3
98.5
```

```
99.2
```

Here is the program that reads these temperatures from the `temperatures.txt` file and prints the average temperature:

```
1   f = open('temperatures.txt', 'r')
2
3   temp1 = float(f.readline())
4   temp2 = float(f.readline())
5   temp3 = float(f.readline())
6   temp4 = float(f.readline())
7
8   avg = (temp1 + temp2 + temp3 + temp4)/4
9   print(avg)
10
11  f.close()
```

Here is the output of this program:

```
94.6
```

Line 1 of this program opens the `temperatures.txt` file for input. It calls the `open()` function to create a file object. Then it assigns the file object to `f`. Line 3 uses the file object to call the `readline()` function to read one line from the input file. Next, it passes the line to the `float()` function to convert it to a float value. Finally, it assigns the float value to the `temp1` variable. Lines 4-6 repeat the process to get the next three float values from the file. Line 8 calculates the average of the four float values and assigns the result to the `avg` variable. Line 9 prints the average. Line 10 calls the `close()` procedure to close the file.

It is possible to read a file *one character a time*. Here is a program that reads the first three characters of the previous `towns.txt` file and prints them out:

```
f = open('towns.txt', 'r')

c = f.read(1)
print(c)

c = f.read(1)
print(c)
```

```
8
9   c = f.read(1)
10  print(c)
11
12  f.close()
```

Here is the output of this program:

```
M
a
r
```

This output is correct, since the first line of the `towns.txt` file is: `Marlboro`. The `read()` function on Line 3 has the parameter `1`. This means it reads one character from the input file. Line 1 stores the character in the variable `c`. Line 4 prints the variable `c`. Lines 6-10 repeat the process to read and print the next two characters of the input file.

The integer parameter of the `read()` function lets you specify how many characters to read. Here is a program that reads the first 12 characters from the `towns.txt` file and prints them out:

```
1  f = open('towns.txt', 'r')
2
3  c = f.read(12)
4  print(c)
5
6  f.close()
```

Here is the output of the program:

```
Marlboro
Man
```

The value `12` on Line 3 tells the `read()` function to read 12 characters from the `towns.txt` file. The twelve characters include the eight characters in `Marlboro`, the invisible newline character, and the three characters in `Man`.

Summary

The ability to accept input in programs is vital. It makes programs more useful and dynamic. Two common ways to accept input are the console and a file. Input gives programs data to process into useful information. Without input, programs would have to *hard-code* data inside programs. That is a very impractical way to provide data. Input data may also help a program decide which path to take. Later examples illustrate demonstrate this.

6 SELECTION

Selection lets programs make decisions. A selection statement defines multiple paths of execution in a program, and it determines which path the program should take. Three common selection statements in programming are If-Then, If-Then-Else, and Switch.

If-Then

The If-Then statement decides if a program should execute a block of code. The If-Then statement starts with a Boolean condition. If its condition is `True`, then the If-Then statement executes its block of code. If its condition is `False`, then the If-Then statement skips its block of code. Here is an example:

```
1  isRaining = True
2  if isRaining:
3      print("Bring an umbrella")
```

Line 1 declares the `isRaining` variable and sets it to `True`. Line 2 uses the `if` keyword to indicate an If-Then statement. A Boolean condition follows the `if` keyword. A colon (`:`) indicates the end of the condition. The program evaluates the condition. Since `isRaining` is the value `True`, the condition evaluates to `True`, and the If-Then statement executes its block of code. The block of code includes the following statements that are indented. In this example, the block of code only contains one statement, the `print()` statement on Line 3. Line 3 is indented four spaces to indicate that it is part of the If-Then block of code. If there were additional statements in the block, they too would be indented four spaces. The program executes the `print()`

statement and `Bring an umbrella` appears in the console window. If instead `isRaining` was `False`, then no console output would appear.

Here is an example of an If-Then statement that has multiple statements in its code block:

```
1  isRaining = True
2  if isRaining:
3      print("Bring an umbrella")
4      print("You might need boots")
5      print("A raincoat might help")
```

In the above program, the three statements on Lines 3-5 are all indented four spaces. Therefore, they are all part of the If-Then block. When the condition on Line 2 is `True`, then Lines 3-5 execute.

The condition of an If-Then statement may be *any* Boolean condition. Here is an example:

```
1  x = 2
2  y = 3
3
4  if x > y:
5      print("x is greater than y")
6
7  if x <= y:
8      print("x is less than or equal to y")
```

Lines 1-2 declare and initialize two variables. The If-Then condition on Line 4 is `False`, so the `print()` statement on Line 5 does not execute. However, the If-Then condition on Line 7 is `True`, so Line 8 executes, and the program outputs `x is less than or equal to y` to the console.

Here is another example that compares String values and has multiple statements in the If-Then block:

```
age = input('How old are you? ')
age = int(age)
if age > 12 and age < 20:
    print("Hello teen!")
    print("You are still a teenager")
```

Here is a sample output of the program:

```
How old are you? 13
Hello teen!
You are still a teenager
```

Line 1 of this program asks the user for an age and accepts the number as input. Line 2 uses the `int()` function to convert the `age` variable to an integer, and it assigns the result back to the `age` variable. The If-Then statement on Line 3 tests if the `age` variable is greater than `12` and less than `20`. If this condition is `True`, then the program executes the If-Then block of statements on Lines 4-5.

If-Then-Else

The If-Then-Else statement is like the If-Then statement, but it also handles the case when the condition is `False`. It provides a block of statements to execute when its condition is `True` and a block of statements to execute when its condition is `False`. Here is an example:

```
1  response = input('What is your age? ')
2
3  if int(response) >= 18:
4      print("You can vote!")
5      print("It's your right!")
6  else:
7      print("You are too young to vote.")
8      print("Wait until you're 18.")
```

Line 1 prompts the user to enter a numeric age, and it stores the input value in the `response` variable. The If-Then-Else statement starts on Line 3. Line 3 uses the `int()` function to convert `response` to an integer, then the condition compares `response` to `18`. If `response` is greater than or equal to `18`, the program executes the block of statements on Lines 4-5. If the condition on Line 3 is `False`, then the program executes the block of statements on Lines 7-8. The If-Then-Else statement provides two paths of execution in the program. The path the program takes depends on the value of its Boolean condition.

Nested If

The If-Then and If-Then-Else constructs are statements. Therefore, you can put them in a code block. Putting an If statement in the block of another If statement is known as *nesting*. For example, you can nest an If-Then-Else statement inside an If-Then-Else statement:

```
1   age = input('What is your age? ')
2   age = int(age)
3   if age > 19:
4       print("Goodbye teen years!")
5       print("It's been real!")
6   else:
7       print("Hello youngster!")
8       if age > 12 and age < 20:
9           print("You are a teenager.")
10          print("Hello teen!")
11      else:
12          print("You are a pre-teen.")
13          print("Hey kid!")
```

Here is a sample output of this program:

```
What is your age? 11
Hello youngster!
You are a pre-teen.
Hey kid!
```

This example demonstrates an If-Then-Else statement that has a nested If-Then-Else statement. Line 1 of this program prompts the user for an age and stores it in the `age` variable. Line 2 converts `age` to an integer and stores it back in the `age` variable. The top-level If-Then-Else statement is on Lines 3-13. If the condition on Line 3 is `True`, then the program executes the block of statements on Lines 4-5. Otherwise, the program executes the block of statements on Lines 7-13. Line 7 prints a string to the console. Lines 8-13 make up the nested If-Then-Else statement. If the condition on Line 8 is `True`, then the program executes the block of statements on Lines 9-10. Otherwise, the program executes the block of statements on Lines 12-13. You can nest any combination of If-Then and If-Then-Else statements. This lets you create intricate decision logic in your programs.

Switch

A single If-Then statement implements one decision path. A single If-

Then-Else statement implements two decision paths. There are times when your program needs more than two decision paths. It is possible to do this with nested If statements, but the programming logic could be complicated and obscure. A Switch statement lets you clearly and succinctly implement more than two decision paths. Although there is no official Switch statement in Python, there is the If-Elif statement. This statement closely resembles Switch statements in other programming languages. Here is a program that accepts a numeric month from the user and displays the month name:

```
month = input('Enter a month number? ')
month = int(month)
if month == 1:
    print("January")
elif month == 2:
    print("February")
elif month == 3:
    print("March")
elif month == 4:
    print("April")
elif month == 5:
    print("May")
elif month == 6:
    print("June")
elif month == 7:
    print("July")
elif month == 8:
    print("August")
elif month == 9:
    print("September")
elif month == 10:
    print("October")
elif month == 11:
    print("November")
elif month == 12:
    print("December")
else:
    print("Invalid month")
```

Here is a sample output of this program:

```
Enter a month number? 5
May
```

Line 1 of this program prompts the user for a numeric month and stores the input value in the **month** variable. Line 2 converts the month variable to an integer. Line 3 checks if **month** is **1**. If so, the program prints **January**, and the If-Elif statement ends. If **month** is not equal to **1**, the program continues to the **elif** clause on Line 5. This checks if **month** is **2**. If it is, Line 6 executes. And so on. There are thirteen possible paths: one case for each numeric month and one default case to catch all invalid months. The program prints the month name for the **month** values **1 - 12**. If the user enters any other number, the program executes the last **else** clause on Line 27 and prints **Invalid month**. Although each of the thirteen cases in this program has only one statement in its block, each block may have multiple statements. Here is an example:

```
bal = 100.00

print("ATM")
print("0 - Make a withdrawal")
print("1 - Make a deposit")
print("2 - Print balance")

choice = int(input('Selection: '))

if choice == 0:
    amt = float(input("Amount to withdraw? "))
    bal = bal - amt;
    print("Balance after withdrawal: " + str(bal))
elif choice == 1:
    amt = float(input("Amount to deposit? "))
    bal = bal + amt;
    print("Balance after deposit: " + str(bal))
elif choice == 2:
    print("Your balance is:")
    print(bal)
else:
    print("Invalid Selection")
```

Here is a sample execution of the program:

```
ATM
0 - Make a withdrawal
1 - Make a deposit
2 - Print balance
Selection: 0
Amount to withdraw? 20
Balance after withdrawal: 80.0
```

Line 1 of this program sets a sample balance value **`100.00`** to the `bal` variable. Lines 3-6 print a user menu to the console. Line 8 prompts the user for a menu selection and passes the result to the `int()` function. The program stores that result in the `choice` variable. Lines 10-22 make up the Switch statement. Line 10 starts the case for processing a withdrawal. If `choice` is equal to `0`, then this is a withdrawal, and the program executes Lines 11-13. Line 11 prompts the user for a withdrawal amount, converts the result to a float, and stores that result in the `amt` variable. Line 12 subtracts `amt` from `bal` and stores the result back in `bal`. Line 13 prints the new balance after the withdrawal. In a similar way, Lines 14-17 process a deposit. Lines 18-20 process a balance inquiry. Lines 21-22 make up the default case that executes when the user enters an invalid menu choice. Interestingly, this basic ATM program allows a user to overdraw from the account and have a negative balance. How would you modify the program to prevent a negative balance? That exercise is left for you!

Summary

Selection statements let programs make decisions. They let programs follow different paths, depending on conditions or values. Three common types of selection statements in programming are the If-Then, If-Then-Else, and Switch statements. Each type of selection statement has a specific purpose, but all the selection statements make programs dynamic. The program may perform differently each time it executes.

7 REPETITION

Repetition is the ability to execute a statement or block of statements multiple times. Programs use **`loops`** to implement repetition. Loops eliminate redundant code, simplify programming, and make programs more maintainable. Two common loops in programming are the For and While loops.

Why Loops?

To understand why loops are necessary, first consider this program that prints `Hello` five times:

```
print("Hello")
print("Hello")
print("Hello")
print("Hello")
print("Hello")
```

The above program is straightforward. However, it is redundant. Maintenance is challenging. Changing the message from `Hello` to `Hello World` would require changing all five lines. Increasing the output from five lines to 1,000 lines would require a lot of typing. When you notice a repetitive behavior in your program, consider using a loop. The next section describes the For loop.

For

The For loop executes a block of code for a specific number of times. It typically uses a sequence of numbers and provides an index variable for the current value of the sequence. Here is a loop that prints the numbers `0, 1, 2, ... , 9`:

```
1  for i in range(0, 10):
2      print(i)
```

Here is the output:

```
0
1
2
3
4
5
6
7
8
9
```

The For loop starts with the `for` keyword on Line 1. The index variable is `i`. The `range()` statement defines a range from `0` to `10`, but not including `10`. The For loop has one `print()` statement in its block. The loop starts on Line 1 by assigning the first value of the range (`0`), to the variable `i`. Then the program executes the `print()` statement to print the current value of `i`. There are no other statements in the loop block, so execution returns to the beginning of the loop on Line 1. The program assigns the next value (`1`) to `i`, and Line 2 prints `i`. This process continues until the last value (`9`) is printed.

Here is a For loop that prints `Hello` five times, while also numbering each line:

```
1  for i in range(0, 5):
2      print( str(i) + ". Hello" )
```

Here is the output:

```
0. Hello
1. Hello
2. Hello
3. Hello
4. Hello
```

Line 2 uses the `str()` function to convert the loop index `i` to a string.

Next, it combines that string to the string `". Hello"` to create a new string. Finally, it prints the new string. This process repeats for each value of the loop index `i`. Changing the loop to print `Hello World` is easy. Just change the string on Line 2:

```
1   for i in range(0, 5):
2       print( str(i) + ". Hello World" )
```

To make the For loop print `Hello World` 1,000 times, change the `5` on Line 1 to **`1000`**:

```
1   for i in range(0, 1000):
2       print( str(i) + ". Hello World" )
```

Unlike the program at the beginning of the chapter, the program above is easier to write and modify. The For loop simplifies the coding and makes the program more maintainable. The previous For loop also demonstrates how a small program can generate lots of output.

A For loop may start with a value other than **`0`**. Here is a For loop that prints the sequence **`100, 101, 102, 103, 104`**:

```
1   for i in range(100, 105):
2       print(i)
```

Here is the output:

```
100
101
102
103
104
```

The previous examples use the **`range()`** statement to define a simple sequence that starts at **`100`**, increases by **`1`**, and ends at **`104`**. The **`range()`** statement has a third parameter that lets you specify the increment step. After each iteration of the loop, the program adds the increment step to the loop index. The increment step determines how the range values changes from iteration to iteration. Omitting this parameter defaults the increment step to `1`. Changing the increment step creates different types of sequences. For example, here is a For loop that prints the sequence `0, 2, 4, 6, 8`:

```
1   for i in range(0, 10, 2):
```

```
    print(i)
```

Here is the output:

```
0
2
4
6
8
```

The first time through this For loop, `i` is `0`. Then the For loop increments `i` by a step value of `2`, and so on. Here is a For loop that prints the sequence `1, 3, 5, 7, 9`:

```
for i in range(1, 10, 2):
    print(i)
```

Here is the output:

```
1
3
5
7
9
```

Simply changing the starting value of the range from `0` to `1` and retaining the step value of `2` generates this sequence of odd numbers. The step value may also be negative. Here is a For loop that prints the sequence `10, 9, 8, ... , 1`:

```
for i in range(10, 0, -1):
    print(i)
```

Here is the output:

```
10
9
8
7
6
5
4
3
```

```
2
1
```

To make this For loop count down, change the starting value of the range to **10**, the ending value to **0**, and the step to **-1**. Setting the starting, ending, and step values of the range lets you define various kinds of sequences.

While

The While loop repeats its statements just like a For loop. However, the While loop repeats its statements while its condition is `True`. Here is a While loop that prints the sequence `0, 1, ... , 9`:

```
1   i = 0
2   while i < 10:
3       print(i)
4       i = i + 1
```

Here is the output:

```
0
1
2
3
4
5
6
7
8
9
```

Line 1 of this program assigns `1` to the variable `i`. The second line is where the While loop starts. It first checks its condition, `i < 10`, to see if it is `True`. Since it is `True`, it executes the two statements in its block, Lines 3-4. Line 3 prints the current value of `i`. Line 4 adds `1` to `i` and assigns the result back to `i`. That completes the first iteration of the loop. The execution goes back to Line 2 to check the condition and determine if the While loop should execute its block again. This process repeats until `i` is `10`. At that point, the condition on Line 2 becomes `False`, and the loop ends. This example shows how While loops are like For loops. But While loops can loop in other ways. Here is a program that accepts grades as input and calculates the average:

```
total = 0.0
```

```
 2  count = 0
 3  grade = float( input('Grade? (-1 to quit): ') )
 4  while (grade >= 0):
 5      total = total + grade
 6      count = count + 1
 7      grade = float( input('Grade? (-1 to quit): ') )
 8
 9  if (count > 0):
10      average = total / count
11      print("Avg. grade: " + str(average) )
```

Here is a sample output:

```
Grade? (-1 to quit):  99.3
Grade? (-1 to quit):  100.0
Grade? (-1 to quit):  98.2
Grade? (-1 to quit):  -1
Avg. grade: 99.16666666666667
```

Line 1 of the program declares and initializes a `total` variable to store the sum of the grades. Line 2 declares and initializes a `count` variable to store the number of grades entered. Line 3 uses the `input()` statement to prompt the user for a grade. The program passes the input value to the `float()` function to convert it to a float value. The program stores the float value in the `grade` variable. The While loop starting on Line 4 checks if the `grade` variable is greater than or equal to `0`. If it is, then the While loop executes its statements on Lines 5-7. Line 5 adds `grade` to `total`. Line 6 increases `count` by `1`. Line 7 prompts the user for another grade. Then, program execution returns to Line 4, and the process repeats. When the user enters a negative grade, the While loop terminates. This is how the user indicates that there are no more grades to input. After the While loop terminates, the program executes the If-Then statement on Lines 9-11. If the user entered at least one grade, then the condition on Line 9 will be `True`, and the If-Then statement executes its block of statements on Lines 10-11. Line 10 calculates the average and stores it in the `average` variable. Line 11 prints `average`. This program shows that While loops are not limited to sequences. While loops can implement repetition for *any* `True`/`False` condition that you create.

Break and Continue

The Break and Continue statements provide two ways to alter the flow of control in loops. Both statements work in For and While loops. The

sections below describe the Break and Continue statements.

Break

When placed inside a loop block, the Break statement forces the program to exit a loop. It lets you terminate a loop immediately. When the program executes a `break` statement inside a loop, execution jumps immediately to the first statement after the loop. Here is an example:

```
1   for i in range(0,10):
2       print(i)
3       if i == 5:
4           Break
5
6   print("bye.")
```

This program has a For loop that repeats 10 times. It prints the value of the loop index `i` each time. However, when `i` is `5`, the If-Then statement in the loop block becomes `True`, and the program executes the `break` statement on Line 4. This forces the For loop to end immediately, effectively skipping the remaining iterations. The last number printed is `5`. Program execution jumps to Line 6 to print the string `"bye."`. Here is the output:

```
0
1
2
3
4
5
bye.
```

The Break statement is useful when a For loop must terminate due to a special case, such as an error condition. Here is an example:

```
sum = 0

for i in range(0, 5):
    grade = input('Grade ' + str(i) + ': ')
    grade = float(grade)
    if grade < 0:
        sum = -1
        print("Invalid Grade")
        break
```

```
10        sum = sum + grade
11
12    if sum != -1:
13        average = sum / 5.0
14        print( "Average: " + str(average) )
```

This program prompts the user to enter five grades and prints the average. But if the user enters a negative number, the program prints an error message and aborts. Line 1 of the program declares a variable named `sum` and sets it to `0`. The For loop is on Lines 3-10. Line 4 accepts a grade from the user and assigns the input value to the `grade` variable. Line 5 uses the `float()` function to convert `grade` to a float value. Then it assigns the float value back to the `grade` variable. The If-Then condition on Line 6 checks if the grade is less than `0`. If it is, then this is an input error, and the program executes its block of statements on Lines 7-9. Line 7 sets the `sum` variable to `-1`. Line 8 prints an error message to the user. Line 9 is a `break` statement. When the program executes the `break` statement, execution jumps from Line 9 to the If-Then statement on Line 12. If the condition on Line 12 is `True`, then the user entered five valid grades. Lines 13-14 calculate and print the average. Here is a sample output when the user enters all valid grades:

```
Grade 0: 100
Grade 1: 89
Grade 2: 91
Grade 3: 87
Grade 4: 99
Average: 93.2
```

Here is a sample output when the user enters an invalid grade, and the `break` statement executes:

```
Grade 0: 100
Grade 1: 98
Grade 2: -99
Invalid Grade
```

Another way to use a Break statement is to break out of an intentionally endless loop. You want to avoid endless loops in your program, and the Break statement is a safeguard. Here is a seemingly endless loop that prints increasing numbers:

```
i = 0
while True:
```

```
3       print(i)
4       i = i + 1
5       if i == 10:
6           break
```

Line 1 of this program declares a variable `i` and initializes it to `0`. The While loop starts on Line 2. Its condition is the literal value `True`, which seems like it will execute its loop block forever. The `print()` statement on Line 3 is the first statement in the loop block. It prints the current value of `i`. Line 4 increases `i` by `1`. The If-Then statement on Lines 5-6 checks if `i` is equal to `10`. If it is, then the `break` statement on Line 6 executes, and the While loop safely terminates. Without Lines 5-6, the program would execute forever. Here is the output of the program:

```
0
1
2
3
4
5
6
7
8
9
```

Continue

The Continue statement is like the Break statement, but it affects loops differently. When placed inside a loop block, the Continue statement immediately forces execution back to the start of the loop for the next iteration. Here is an example:

```
print("Odd numbers:")
for i in range(0, 10):
    if i % 2 == 0:
        continue
    print(i)
```

Here is the output:

```
Odd numbers:
1
3
```

```
5
7
9
```

This program prints the odd numbers from `0` to `9`. The If-Then statement on Line 3 checks if `i` is divisible by `2`; if it is, then `i` is an even number, and the program executes the `continue` statement on Line 4. This forces execution back to the start of the loop on Line 2, and the For loop increases `i` for the next iteration. The `continue` statement effectively skips the remaining statements in the loop block. In this case, Line 5 is the only remaining statement in the loop block. In general, the `continue` statement skips any following statements in a loop block and jumps back to the start of the loop for the next iteration. This is a way to skip the remaining statements in a loop block, when it does not make sense to execute them.

The Break and Continue statements modify the flow of execution in a loop. They work in both For and While loops, and they apply to the immediately surrounding loop. The Break and Continue statements have different purposes. Use the Break statement to immediately exit a loop. Use the Continue statement to immediately return to the start of the loop.

Summary

Programs use repetition to simplify coding tasks. Repetition makes programs more maintainable. The For and While loops implement repetition in programming. Each type of loop executes a block of statements for some number of times. Loops use conditions to determine when they should stop executing. Loops are useful, because they let programs do a lot of work with a small amount of code. Without loops, programs would be redundant and difficult to maintain. Some programming tasks would not be possible without loops.

8 LISTS

Programs frequently need to store multiple values for the same type of data. For example, consider the following program that stores five grades:

```
grade0 = 99
grade1 = 84
grade2 = 100
grade3 = 92
grade4 = 87
```

Although this program is valid, there are a few concerns. First, the program is redundant; it requires five similar lines of code to store the five grades. Next, the program is inflexible. What if the program needs to store 10 grades? The program currently cannot handle that. Finally, the program is tedious; imagine storing 1,000 grades. That would require a lot of code.

This situation calls for a Python *list*. This is an important programming concept that is common in most programming languages. The Python list is an advanced form of the classic *array* concept. This chapter discusses the list concept, single-dimensional lists, and multidimensional lists.

List

A list is a group of variables that have the same *name* and *type*. Although Python lists may contain different types of data, this chapter focuses on classic lists that only have one type of data. Each variable of the list is known as an *element* of the list. To access a particular element of the list, use its integer index. The first element of the list is at index `0`, the second element of the list is at index `1`, and so on. A list has a length, which is a count of the number of elements in the list. Here is an example that stores five grades using a list:

```
1   grade = [ 99 , 84 , 100 , 92 , 87 ]
2
3   print(grade[0])    # 99
4   print(grade[4])    # 87
5
6   print(len(grade)) # 5
7
8   grade[0] = 111
9   print(grade[0])    # 111
```

Line 1 of this program creates a list named `grade` that has a length of `5`, and it initializes the list with five integer values. The valid indexes of the array are `0`, `1`, `2`, `3`, and `4`. Line 3 uses index `0` to access the first element of the list and print it. To access a specific element of a list, specify an integer index in square brackets (`[]`) after the list name. Line 4 uses index `4` to access the last element of the list and print it. Line 6 uses the `len()` function to return the length of the `grade` list. The `len()` function accepts a list as a parameter and returns the length of that list. Line 8 uses index `0` to change the first element of the list to `111`. Line 9 uses index `0` to print the first element of the list. Here is the output of the program:

```
99
87
5
111
```

Since the list index is an integer sequence, lists work well with loops. Combining lists with loops is a common practice in programming. Here is a For loop that prints each element of a list:

```
1   grade = [ 99 , 84 , 100 , 92 , 87 ]
2   for i in range( 0, len(grade) ):
3       print(grade[i])
```

Line 1 of this program creates and initializes the list `grade`. Lines 2-3 make up the For loop to print every element of the list. Notice how the For loop index `i` starts at `0` and ends at the length of the `grade` list minus `1`; it is the sequence `0`, `1`, `2`, `3`, `4`. That sequence contains every index of the `grade` list, in increasing order. No matter how big the `grade` list is, the program only needs two lines to print every element. Even if you change the size of the grade list, the For loop will still work.

The **append()** list method adds an element to the end of the list and increases the list length by one. Here is an example:

```
1  grade = [ 99 , 84 , 100 , 92 , 87 ]
2
3  grade.append(88)
4
5  print(grade[5]) # 88
6  print(len(grade)) # 6
```

This example shows how lists are more flexible than plain variables. The **append()** method lets the list grow as needed. Line 3 of the program calls the **append()** method to add the integer value **88** to the end of the list. Use the list and a dot (**.**) symbol to invoke the **append()** method on a list. Pass the item to be added as a parameter to the **append()** method. Line 5 prints the new last element of the list. Line 6 prints the new length of the list.

Now it possible to let the user choose how many grades to enter. Here is an example:

```
grade = []

count = input('Number of grades? ')
count = int(count)
for i in range( 0, count ):
    val = input('Grade ' + str(i) +': ')
    val = int(val)
    grade.append( val )

for i in range( 0, len(grade) ):
    print(grade[i])
```

Here is a sample run of the program:

```
Number of grades? 5
Grade 0: 99
Grade 1: 88
Grade 2: 77
Grade 3: 66
Grade 4: 55
```

```
99
88
77
66
55
```

This program demonstrates several useful features of the Python list. Line 1 creates an empty list (`[]`) and assigns it to the **grade** variable. Line 3 asks the user to input the number of grades to enter and stores the value in the variable `count`. This makes the program dynamic, since the user can specify any number of grades. Line 4 converts the `count` variable to an integer. Lines 5-8 specify a For loop to accept the desired number of grades. The loop index `i` on Line 5 goes from `0` to the `count` variable. Since the user inputs the `count` variable, the user determines the list size. Line 6 prompts the user to enter a value for a grade. The prompt string uses the For loop index `i` to ask for a particular grade number. Line 7 converts the grade to an integer. Line 8 uses the `append()` method to add that value at the end of the list. This process repeats until the user enters all the grades. Lines 10-11 use a For loop to print each element of the list.

Combining a list with a For loop simplifies processing. Here is a program that calculates the average grade:

```
1  grade = [ 99, 98, 82, 70, 100, 91, 85 ]
2
3  total = 0.0
4  for i in range( 0, len(grade) ):
5      total = total + grade[i]
6
7  avg = total / len(grade)
8
9  print('Average: ' + str(avg)) # 89.2857142857
```

The For loop in this program conveniently sums all the grades in the `grade` list. Line 1 creates and initializes a list named `grade`. Line 3 declares a variable named `total` and initializes it to `0.0`. The For loop on Lines 4-5 accesses each element of the list and adds it to the `total` variable. Line 7 calculates the average by dividing the total by the size of the `grade` list. Line 9 prints the average.

When you need to access all elements of a list, whether to read or assign a value, use a For loop to simplify the process.

Two-Dimensional List

A *two-dimensional* list is a list of lists. In other words, it is a list where each element is also a list. There are many examples of two-dimensional lists in the real world. Tic Tac Toe and chess boards are two-dimensional lists. A spreadsheet is another example. If an item has rows and columns, you can use a two-dimensional list to represent it.

Here is an example to create a Tic Tac Toe board as a two-dimensional list and print it:

```
1  board = [
2     ['O','O','X'],
3     ['X','O','O'],
4     ['X','X','X']
5  ]
6
7  print(board)
```

The left square bracket (`[`) on Line 1 is the start of the two-dimensional list. The right square bracket (`]`) on Line 5 is the end of the two-dimensional list. Lines 2-4 are the elements of the two-dimensional list. Each element is also a list, surrounded by `[` and `]`, and separated by commas. For example, the first element of the two-dimensional list is the list `['O','O','X']`. The output of this program shows a list with three elements, where each element is also a list:

```
[['O', 'O', 'X'], ['X', 'O', 'O'], ['X', 'X', 'X']]
```

Since there are two dimensions in the two-dimensional list, accessing a single character requires two indexes: row and column. The row specifies which list, and the column specifies which character within that list. For example, the middle space on this Tic Tac Toe board is at the second row and second column. Since array indexes start at `0`, the middle space is the element at: `board[1][1]`. The number in the first set of square brackets (`[]`) is the row index. The number in the second set of square brackets is the column index. The middle `'X'` character of the last row is the element at `board[2][1]`. To access one of the lists in the two-dimensional list, simply leave off the last index. For example, `board[1]` is the second list. Here is a complete example:

```
board = [
   ['O','O','X'],
```

```
3     ['X','O','O'],
4     ['X','X','X']
5   ]
6
7   print(board[1][1]) # center
8   print(board[2][0]) # bottom left
9   print(board[0][2]) # top right
10  print(board[1]) # middle row
11  print(len(board[1])) # length of second row
12  print(len(board)) # length of board
```

The first three `print()` statements on Lines 7-9 print the contents of the center, bottom left, and top right values of the board. The `print()` statement on Line 10 prints the entire second row of the board. The `print()` statement on Line 11 prints the length of that row; there are three characters in that row (list), so the output is `3`. The `print()` statement on Line 12 prints the length of the board; this board has three lists (elements), so the output is `3`.

Since there are two indexes in a two-dimensional list, you need two loops to iterate over all the elements. The first loop iterates through the rows (lists). The second loop iterates through the elements of each row. The second loop is nested inside the first loop. Here is an example to print all the elements of the board, row by row:

```
board = [
  ['O','O','X'],
  ['X','O','O'],
  ['X','X','X']
]

for row in range( 0, len(board) ):
    str = ""
    for col in range(0, len(board[row]) ):
        str = str + board[row][col] + " "
    print(str)
```

Here is the output of the program:

```
O O X
X O O
```

```
X X X
```

Two `for` loops are required to print each element of the board. For each row, the program reads each column of that row. The outer `for` loop is on Lines 7-11. This loop provides the row index `row`. The inner `for` loop is on Lines 9-10. This inner For loop provides the column index `col`. Line 10 accesses each element of the board by using the current row and column indexes and concatenates the element to the `str` variable. When the inner `for` loop completes, the `str` variable has an entire row of data. The next statement after the inner For loop (Line 11) prints the `str` variable, and the program returns to the top of the outer `for` loop (Line 7) to get the next row index. This process repeats until the program prints all the rows.

To determine if there is a Tic Tac Toe row winner, the program must compare the elements of each row for equality. Here is an example:

```
1   board = [
2     ['O','O','X'],
3     ['X','O','O'],
4     ['X','X','X']
5   ]
6
7   row_winner = False
8   for row in range( 0, len(board) ):
9       if (board[row][0] == board[row][1] and
10          board[row][0] == board[row][2]):
11          row_winner = True
12          break
13
14  print("Row winner? " + str(row_winner))
```

Lines 1-5 declare a variable named `board` and assign a two-dimensional list to it. Line 7 of this program declares a Boolean variable named `row_winner` and initializes it to `False`. The For loop on Lines 8-12 loops through each row of the board. The If-Then condition on Lines 9-10 compares the first element of the row with the second element of the row for equality. Then it compares the first element of the row with the third element of the row for equality. If both comparisons are `True`, then all elements of the current row are equal, and the program executes Line 11 to set the `row_winner` variable to `True`. The Break statement on Line 12 breaks out of the loop, and execution continues to the `print()` statement on Line 14 to print the value of `row_winner`. Other comparisons can determine column and diagonal winners as well. Those are good practice exercises for you.

Multidimensional Lists

Lists may be greater than two dimensions. These multidimensional lists require an additional index for each additional dimension. Otherwise, multidimensional lists work the same way. Just know when you are working with a single element, a single list, a list of lists, a list of lists of lists, and so on. Try working with a three-dimensional list for practice.

Summary

Lists are a way to easily define and access a group of variables. In the classic list, each variable has the same name and same type. To access a specific element of the list, use the integer index. The first element of the list is at index `0`. The common variable name and the index make it easy to access all the variables, particularly with the For loop. When programs need to declare many related variables, all with the same type, consider using a list.

9 MODULAR PROGRAMMING

Modular programming is a way to write programs in a simpler and more organized manner. Instead of creating one large program, the modular approach breaks the program into small, more manageable sub-programs. The following sections describe the benefits of modular programming and how to implement this approach in your programs.

Why Go Modular?

There are many reasons why to use a modular programming approach. Here are a few:

1. **Divide-and-Conquer**. Breaking up a programming task into sub-programs lets multiple programmers work on the same program at the same time. Programmers independently focus on their own modules and integrate their code later. This speeds up program development.
2. **Simpler Development**. It is easier to write a short and simple program than a large and complicated one. When a programming task is complicated, it helps to break it up into smaller, more manageable sub-programs.
3. **Simpler Debugging**. It is easier to debug a small program than a large one. In a small program, there are less statements to check for errors. There are fewer requirements to verify and validate.
4. **Code Reuse**. A reusable module eliminates duplicate code. It encourages code reuse when a program must call the same functionality in multiple places.
5. **Easier Maintenance**. If the requirements of a module change, then only the module must change. Every other place in the

program that calls the module does *not* have to change. Each place gets the update immediately, since the change occurs in one common module.

Writing Modules

A module in a single program may be a *function* or a *procedure*. A function performs some logic and returns a result. A procedure performs some logic, but it does not return a result. The following sections describe these two types of modules and provide examples.

Functions

A function is a type of module that returns a value. It is a user-defined module that performs some job and returns a result. A function is useful, because you may define it once and use it multiple times. Consider this program that converts four different Fahrenheit temperatures to Celsius:

```
f = 90.0
c = (f - 32.0) * 5.0/9.0
print(c)

f = 72.5
c = (f - 32.0) * 5.0/9.0
print(c)

f = 86.4
c = (f - 32.0) * 5.0/9.0
print(c)

f = 55.2
c = (f - 32.0) * 5.0/9.0
print(c)
```

Here is the output:

```
32.2222222222
22.5
30.2222222222
12.8888888889
```

You can see the disadvantages in the program above. It is repetitive and tedious. The same calculation appears multiple times. There is a possibility of an error each time you type the calculation. Here is an example of the previous program, but with a function:

```
1   def fahrToCels(f):
2       c = (f - 32.0) * 5.0/9.0
3       return c
4
5   print( fahrToCels(90.0) )
6   print( fahrToCels(72.5) )
7   print( fahrToCels(86.4) )
8   print( fahrToCels(55.2) )
```

Lines 1-3 of this program define a function named `fahrToCels`. The `def` keyword indicates a function definition. The `f` variable in parentheses indicates an input parameter to the function. In other words, when you call the function, you must pass it one value. In this case, `f` represents the Fahrenheit temperature to convert to Celsius. Lines 2-3 are the function body. The indenting is important in Python. Line 2 is a calculation to convert the Fahrenheit temperature to Celsius. Line 3 uses the `return` statement to return the result. A function must execute a `return` statement before completing. The first three lines make up the definition. No processing occurs in the program at this point. Line 5 calls the function, while passing it the parameter `90.0`. The function definition on Lines 2-3 execute, with `f` having the value `90.0`. Line 2 performs the calculation. Line 3 returns the result. Line 5 receives the result (`90.0`), and it prints it to the console. Lines 6-8 make three more calls to the function and print the results. The output of this program is the same as the previous program.

The advantages of this modular program are apparent. Using a function reduces the amount of code. The code is simpler and less error-prone, since it only specifies the calculation once. If there is a problem with the calculation, there is only one place to fix it. Performing additional temperature conversions is easy. Just make more calls to the function.

Here is another example. This function accepts three integer parameters and returns the largest of the three:

```
def max(x,y,z):
    if (x >= y and x >= z):
        return x
    elif (y >= x and y >= z):
        return y
    else:
```

```
 7            return z
 8
 9   print( max(1,2,3) ) # prints 3
10   print( max(5,9,8) ) # prints 9
11   print( max(7,7,6) ) # prints 7
```

Lines 1-7 are the function definition. The selection statement on Lines 2-7 compares the three parameters to find the largest and returns that value. If the condition on Line 2 is `True`, then the function returns `x` as the largest value. Otherwise, if the condition on Line 4 is `True`, then the function returns `y` as the largest value. If neither of those conditions is True, then the function reaches Line 7 to return `z` as the largest value. Lines 9-11 make three calls to the `max` function and print the results. Once again, this example reduces the amount of code by using a function.

Here is an example of a function that sums consecutive numbers:

```
 1   def sum_consecutive_nums(n):
 2       total = 0
 3       for i in range(0, n+1):
 4           total = total + i
 5
 6       return total
 7
 8   print( sum_consecutive_nums(5) )  # 15
 9   print( sum_consecutive_nums(11) ) # 66
10   print( sum_consecutive_nums(32) ) # 528
```

Line 1 of this program declares a function named `sum_consecutive_nums` that accepts an integer parameter `n`. Lines 2-6 are the function body. Line 2 declares a variable named `total` to store the sum of the consecutive numbers from `0` to `n`. Lines 3-4 declare a For loop from `0` to `n+1`. This range represents the consecutive numbers from `0` to `n`. The For loop executes one statement, Line 4. Line 4 adds the current value of the For loop index `i` to the `total` variable. After the For loop, the function executes Line 6 to return the `total` variable. Lines 8-10 are the main section of the program. These three lines make three calls to the function, with three different parameters, and print the results.

Now imagine that a programmer improves the `sum_consecutive_nums` function with a more efficient algorithm. Only the function definition needs to change:

```
1   def sum_consecutive_nums(n):
2       return ( n * (n+1) )/2
3
4   print( sum_consecutive_nums(5) )  # 15
5   print( sum_consecutive_nums(11) ) # 66
6   print( sum_consecutive_nums(32) ) # 528
```

Lines 1-2 are the improved function. The equation on Line 2 is a faster way to sum the consecutive numbers from `0` to `n`. Lines 4-6 automatically benefit from the more efficient function, yet these lines did not have to change at all.

Procedures

A procedure is a type of module that does *not* return a value. Use a procedure to define repetitive behavior that does not need to return a result. Here is an example of a procedure that outputs a square shape to the console:

```
1   def square(len):
2       str = ''
3       for i in range(0, len):
4           for j in range(0, len):
5               str = str + '* '
6           print(str)
7           str = ''
8
9   square(5)
```

Here is the output:

```
* * * * *
* * * * *
* * * * *
* * * * *
* * * * *
```

Lines 1-7 are the definition for a procedure named **`square`**. Note that there is no **`return`** statement in this procedure definition. This procedure accepts a **`len`** parameter that represents the length of the square to draw. The For loop and nested For loop in the definition output rows of `'*'` characters of length **`len`**. Line 9 calls the procedure to output a square of length **`5`**. All the work occurs inside the procedure definition. However, procedures have the same advantages as functions. Here is a variation of the previous program:

```
def square(len):
    str = ''
    for i in range(0, len):
        for j in range(0, len):
            str = str + '* '
        print(str)
        str = ''

square(5)
square(7)
square(8)
square(3)
square(10)
square(11)
square(5)
square(4)
square(6)
square(2)
```

In this example, the program calls the `square` procedure 10 times to output 10 squares of different sizes. The procedure simplifies the code by defining the logic in one place. The program calls the procedure multiple times to output several squares of different sizes.

Procedures are helpful when multiple statements must execute often. Here is an example of an ATM menu:

```
def print_atm_menu():
    print("Welcome to the ATM!")
    print("1. Withdraw")
    print("2. Deposit")
    print("3. Transfer")
    print("4. Balance Inquiry")

print_atm_menu()
```

Here is the output:

```
Welcome to the ATM!
1. Withdraw
2. Deposit
3. Transfer
4. Balance Inquiry
```

The `print_atm_menu` procedure prints a menu to the console. Line 1 defines the procedure name and parameters. In this case, there are no parameters; procedures and functions do not have to accept input parameters. Lines 2-6 are the `print` statements that output the menu. The procedure is useful, because you do not have to execute the five `print` statements every time you want to display the menu. Instead, you may simply call the procedure like in Line 8.

Scoping

Most of the previous program examples in this chapter use parameters to pass data to functions and procedures. Another way to make data visible to a module is through *global* scope. In other words, you can make variables declared outside of the module visible inside the module. Here is an example:

```
 1  sum = 10
 2
 3  def add1(x):
 4      global sum
 5      sum += x
 6
 7  def add2(x):
 8      sum = 0
 9      sum += x
10
11  add1(20)
12  add2(30)
13  add1(40)
14  add2(50)
15
16  print(sum) # 70
```

Line 1 of this program declares the `sum` variable and initializes it to `10`. Lines 3-5 declare a procedure named `add1()` that accepts a parameter `x`. Line 4 uses the `global` keyword to indicate that the `sum` variable is declared outside of this procedure. That means it references the **sum** variable declared on Line 1. Line 5 adds the parameter **x** to the global variable **sum**. Lines 7-9 declare a procedure named **add2()** that accepts a parameter **x**. Since Line 8 does *not* use the **global** keyword, Line 8 is a *new* variable named **sum** that is only accessible inside the **add2()** procedure. Any change to the **sum** variable inside the **add2()** procedure does *not* affect the **sum** variable on Line 1. Line 9 adds the parameter **x** to the local variable **sum** on Line 8. Lines11-14 make three calls to the **add1()** and **add2()** procedures, passing in different values. Line 16 prints the final value of the **sum** variable on Line 1. Only the calls to the **add1()** procedure affect the **sum** variable on Line 1. After Line 11 executes, **sum** is **30**. After Line 12 executes, **sum** is still **30**. After Line 13 executes, **sum** is **70**. After Line 14 executes, **sum** is still **70**. Line 16 prints the final value of **sum**: **70**.

Big Modular Example

The final example of the chapter emphasizes the power of the modular approach. The program defines several procedures and functions to let users explore squares. Here is the code for the Square Program:

```
def print_menu():
    print("Welcome to the Square Program!")
    print("1. Print Square")
    print("2. Calculate Area")
    print("3. Help")
    print("4. Quit")
    print("")

def process_choice(n):
    if (n == 1):
        user_len = get_length()
        print_square(user_len)
    elif (n == 2):
        user_len = get_length()
        area = calculate_area(user_len)
        print("")
        print("The area is: " + str(area) )
        print("")
    elif (n == 3):
        help()
```

```
    elif (n == 4):
        print("Bye.")
    else:
        print("Invalid selection.")

def print_square(len):
    print("")
    str = ''
    for i in range(0, len):
        for j in range(0, len):
            str = str + '* '
        print(str)
        str = ''
    print("")

def calculate_area(n):
    return( n * n )

def get_length():
    square_len = -1
    while(square_len < 0):
        square_len = int( input('Enter length: ') )
        if (square_len < 0):
            print("Error - invalid length")
    return square_len

def help():
    str = "\n"
    str += "Welcome to the Square Program! "
    str += "You can do three things. "
    str += "You can print a graphical square. "
    str += "You can calculate the area of a square. "
    str += "You can print this help menu. "
    str += "We hope you enjoy this program!"
    str += "\n"
    print(str)

```

```
# main
response = -1
while (True):
    print_menu()
    response = int( input('Your choice? ') )
    process_choice(response)
    if (response == 4):
        break
```

Here is a sample output for this program:

```
Welcome to the Square Program!
1. Print Square
2. Calculate Area
3. Help
4. Quit

Your choice? 3

Welcome to the Square Program! You can do three things.
You can print a graphical square. You can calculate the
area of a square. You can print this help menu. We hope
you enjoy this program!

Welcome to the Square Program!
1. Print Square
2. Calculate Area
3. Help
4. Quit

Your choice? 1
Enter length: 4

* * * *
* * * *
* * * *
* * * *

Welcome to the Square Program!
1. Print Square
2. Calculate Area
3. Help
4. Quit
```

```
Your choice? 2
Enter length: 3

The area is: 9

Welcome to the Square Program!
1. Print Square
2. Calculate Area
3. Help
4. Quit

Your choice? 4
Bye.
```

This program uses both procedures and functions to take a modular approach to this program. Lines 1-56 define several procedures and functions. Lines 59-65 define the main logic of the program. Line 59 is where program execution starts. Using modules makes the main part of the program simple, clear, and easy to understand. The main logic has a While loop that lets the user access the menu over and over. Line 61 calls the `print_menu()` procedure to output the program menu. Line 63 calls the `process_choice()` procedure to process the user choice. The user choice is a parameter to the `process_choice()` procedure. Lines 9-24 define the `process_choice()` procedure. This procedure demonstrates that you can call procedures and functions from inside a procedure or function. The `process_choice()` procedure calls the `get_length()` function on Line 11 and Line 14 to get the length of a square from the user. It calls the `print_square()` procedure on Line 12 to print a graphical square. Finally, it calls the `calculate_area()` function on Line 15 to calculate and print the area of a square.

The example shows how you can divide a large task into smaller ones. The process is like creating an outline for a term paper. You think about the structure of the paper, the different parts, the order, how the parts work together, and more. The procedures and functions implement different tasks of the program. Once these individual parts are working, you can organize and integrate them to complete the overall task.

Summary

The programming examples in this chapter demonstrate the many benefits of modular programming. To implement modular programming in your programs, define functions and procedures for repetitive or complicated programming logic. Use modular programming to divide and conquer your programs. The modular approach will make it easier to develop difficult programs.

10 USING LIBRARIES

Programming languages often provide libraries of code for you to use. These libraries are built-in, proven code modules that implement useful programming functions and procedures. This chapter discusses how to access and use libraries in Python.

Accessing Libraries

The Import Statement

Before using a Python library, you must tell the program to include it. The `import` statement specifies a library to include. You may include multiple libraries in your Python programs. Here is an example that includes and uses the `math` library:

```
1   import math
2
3   x = math.factorial(4)
4   print(x)
```

Line 1 of this program imports the `math` library into the program. Line 3 accesses and uses the `factorial()` function to calculate the factorial of `4`. Note that the program must use the `math.` prefix to access the `factorial()` function. You can expect the `factorial()` function to work correctly, since Python provides it to you in the `math` library. It is not necessary to create a `factorial()` function of your own.

The From Statement

Another way to use a Python library is to use the `from` statement to import an item from a module. Here is an example:

```
1   from datetime import date
2
3   d = date.today()
4   print(d)
```

Line 1 of this program imports `date` from the `datetime` module. Line 3 calls the `today()` function to retrieve the current date in the form YYYY-MM-DD. Line 4 prints the date.

More Examples

Here are more examples of libraries you can use. One useful feature of programming languages is the ability to generate random numbers:

```
1   from random import randint
2
3   num = randint(0,9)
4   print(num)
```

Line 1 of this program imports `randint` from the `random` module. The `randint()` function on Line 3 returns a random integer from `0` to `9` (including both `0` and `9`). The program assigns the result to the `num` variable. Line 4 prints the `num` variable. Random numbers are useful in games or simulations.

The `os` module provides methods and properties related to the operating system. Here is a program that uses the `os` module:

```
1   import os
2
3   print(os.name)
4   print(os.getcwd())
```

Line 1 of this program imports the `os` module. Line 3 accesses the `name` property of the `os` module to retrieve the operating system dependent module. Then it prints the property. Line 4 invokes the `getcwd()` function of the `os` module to get the current working directory. Then it prints the current working directory

Here is an example that uses the `time` module:

```
import time
```

```
2
3   print("Before")
4
5   time.sleep(5)
6
7   print("After")
```

Line 2 of this program prints `"Before"` to the console. Line 3 calls the `sleep()` procedure of the `time` module to pause program execution for 5 seconds. After 5 seconds, the program resumes at Line 7 and prints `"After"` to the console.

The built-in *array* class is an efficient array of numeric values. It is similar to the Python list. Here is an example:

```
1   from array import array

2   arr1 = array('l', [10, 20, 30, 40, 50, 60])

3   print(arr1[0]) # 10
4   print(arr1[2]) # 30
5   print(len(arr1)) # 60
6   print(arr1.itemsize) # 4 bytes
```

Line 1 of this program imports the built-in `array` library. Line 2 calls the `array()` function to create the list `[10, 20, 30, 40, 50, 60]` of type *signed long* (`'l'`). In other words, each element of the list is of type *signed long* (`'l'`). Line 3 prints the first element of the array. Line 4 prints the third element of the array. Line 5 prints the array length. Line 6 prints the size of a single item in the array.

Python Package Index (PyPI)

Although there are many built-in libraries that come with Python, these libraries cannot address all the specific needs of users. Another benefit of Python is the ability to create and publish your own libraries. The Python Package Index (PyPI) is a public repository of user-defined libraries. You can access PyPI from your web browser: https://pypi.org/ . There are lots of useful libraries of functions, procedures, and properties for a variety of applications. There are libraries for statistical calculations, file parsing, web development, and more. Before coding custom programming logic from scratch, check PyPI to see if the logic already exists. Chances are it does.

Summary

There are many built-in and user-defined Python libraries available to you. These libraries offer many proven functions, procedures, and properties for common programming tasks. Libraries simplify and speed up programming development. Before you write a function or procedure, see if it already exists in a library. That will save you time and effort. Why reinvent the wheel?

11 PUTTING IT ALL TOGETHER

The previous chapters explained important concepts that programmers should know. It takes time and practice to know when and how to apply these concepts in your programs. This chapter walks through a few sample programs that leverage the programming concepts from this book. The programs are larger than the previous examples, and they require many of the programming concepts in this book.

The Rainfall Problem

In 1986, Elliot Soloway published the *rainfall problem*[1], a programming task that measured how well students combined and used programming concepts. The rainfall problem is as follows: *Read in integers that represent daily rainfall, and print out the average daily rainfall; if the input value of rainfall is less than zero, prompt the user for a new rainfall.* The problem explicitly states a few programming concepts: input, output, and arithmetic operations. The problem suggests a need for a loop. The following paragraphs show how to leverage several programming concepts to solve the rainfall problem.

Welcome Message

The program begins with a message to the user. The first two lines of the program are a comment and a `print()` statement to welcome the user:

```
# A program to solve Soloway's Rainfall Problem
print("Welcome to the Rainfall Program!")
```

---

[1] E. Soloway. Learning to program = learning to construct mechanisms and explanations. Communications of the ACM, 29(9):850–858, Sept. 1986.

Variables

The program needs a few variables to track the sum of all rainfall amounts and a count of rainfall amounts. The program could use a list to simplify the process. However, this solution uses variables to illustrate the considerations of this problem. Here are the two variables for this program:

```
total = 0.0
count = 0
```

The **total** variable holds a float value, since the average calculation must output decimal places. The **count** variable is an integer amount.

Single Input

The next step is to ask the user for a daily rainfall amount in inches. The program gets a single input for now. Later, the program will incorporate a loop to get more rainfall amounts. Here is the code:

```
rainfall = int( input('Rainfall amount? ') )
```

This statement prompts the user to enter a single rainfall amount and stores that input value in the **rainfall** variable. The **input()** statement accepts and returns the input value. The surrounding **int()** function takes the return value from the **input()** statement and converts it to an integer.

Validating Input

The next step is to ensure that the input value is nonnegative. To achieve this, the program must continue to loop until the user enters a valid value. The loop will output an error message for invalid values and prompt the user to reenter the daily rainfall amount. Here is the code:

```
while rainfall < 0:
    print("Error. Rainfall must be >= 0")
    rainfall = int(input('Rainfall amount? '))
```

Here is a sample run:

```
Welcome to the Rainfall Program!
Rainfall amount? -1
Error. Rainfall must be >= 0
Rainfall amount? -2
Error. Rainfall must be >= 0
Rainfall amount? 4
```

The **while** loop is an excellent choice for this validation. It checks the initial input from the user. If the amount is negative, then it prints an error and executes another input statement. The program continues to execute this **while** loop until the user inputs a nonnegative rainfall amount. When the program completes the **while** loop, the **rainfall** variable will contain a nonnegative number. At this point, the program has successfully accepted one valid rainfall amount from the user. Note that the program still needs a way to stop accepting valid rainfall amounts from the user. The next section addresses that.

Updating Variables

At this point in the program, the **rainfall** variable has a valid rainfall amount. So immediately after the validation **while** loop, the program updates the **total** and **count** variables:

```
total = total + rainfall
count = count + 1
```

Multiple Rainfall Input

So far, the program successfully retrieves a valid rainfall amount from the user and updates variables. But this process may occur multiple times. The program must allow the user to enter multiple rainfall values. By nesting the previous code inside another loop, the program can accept multiple valid rainfall values. This new outer loop will need a way to terminate. An effective way to signal the end of input is to let the user input a known terminating value. **99999** is a good terminating value, since 99,999 inches of rain in one day is not likely to happen. Also, **99999** is a valid nonnegative value, so the current program will accept it. Here is the full program with the new code to accept multiple, valid rainfall values:

```
# A program to solve Soloway's Rainfall Problem
print("Welcome to the Rainfall Program!")

total = 0
count = 0
rainfall = 0

while rainfall != 99999:
    rainfall = int(input('Rainfall amount? '))

    while rainfall < 0:
```

```
12          print("Error. Rainfall must be >= 0")
13          rainfall=int(input('Rainfall amount? '))
14
15      total = total + rainfall
16      count = count + 1
```

There are a few changes here. First, the program initializes the `rainfall` variable on Line 6 to 0. The new `while` loop on Line 8 encloses the previous code to accept a valid rainfall amount from the user. Since the `rainfall` variable initially contains `0`, then the outer `while` loop will execute its block of statements at least one time. Its loop block executes as before, accepting a valid nonnegative rainfall amount from the user.

There is an issue with the current program. If the user enters `99999`, then the program should ignore that value and avoid updating the variables on Lines 15-16. This value also signals the end of input, so the program should exit the outer while loop immediately, since the user does not want to enter any more rainfall amounts. An If-Then-Else statement around the variables implements this behavior:

```
    if (rainfall != 99999):
        total = total + rainfall
        count = count + 1
    else:
        break
```

Displaying the Result

After the user finishes entering rainfall amounts, the program calculates the average and displays the result. One condition to check for is the case where the user did not enter any valid values. If the `count` variable is `0` at the end of the program, then the user entered zero values. An If-Then-Else statement at the end of the program allows the program to either inform the user that there were no input values or calculate and display the average daily rainfall. Here is the If-Then-Else statement at the end of the program:

```
if count > 0:
    average = total / count
    print("Average rainfall: " + str(average))
else:
    print("No input values.")
```

Now the program fulfills all of the requirements of the rainfall problem.

Source Code

Here is a complete listing of the rainfall program:

```
# A program to solve Soloway's Rainfall Problem
print("Welcome to the Rainfall Program!")

total = 0.0
count = 0
rainfall = 0

while rainfall != 99999:
    rainfall = int(input('Rainfall amount? '))

    while rainfall < 0:
        print("Error. Rainfall must be >= 0")
        rainfall=int(input('Rainfall amount? '))

    if (rainfall != 99999):
        total = total + rainfall
        count = count + 1
    else:
        break

if count > 0:
    average = total / count
    print("Average rainfall: " + str(average))
else:
    print("No input values.")
```

Here is a sample run of the program:

```
Welcome to the Rainfall Program!
Rainfall amount? 1
Rainfall amount? 2
Rainfall amount? -9
Error. Rainfall must be >= 0
Rainfall amount? 3
Rainfall amount? 4
```

```
Rainfall amount? 5
Rainfall amount? 6
Rainfall amount? 99999
Average rainfall: 3.5
```

Discussion

The solution to the rainfall problem requires an understanding of several basic programming concepts such as input, output, arithmetic operations, selection, and loops. It requires knowing when and how to use these concepts. A programmer must know how to combine these concepts to solve the problem. A step by step approach breaks down the problem into smaller tasks that are easier to solve. The rainfall problem is challenging for beginners but solving programming problems like this one becomes easier with experience.

Rock, Scissors, Paper

Rock, Scissors, Paper is a game for two players. Each player secretly chooses either rock, scissors, or paper, then reveals the choice. The winner is determined as follows: 1) rock beats scissors, 2) scissors beats paper, and 3) paper beats rock. If both players reveal the same item, then the game is a tie. The goal of this program is to allow a human to play against the computer in a game of Rock, Scissors, Paper.

Assumptions

Here are the assumptions of the program:

1. The winner is the first player (either human or computer) to win 3 out of 5 games.
2. The human will enter `0` for rock, `1` for scissors, and `2` for paper.
3. If the human enters any other number, the program will print an error message and ask the human to try again.

Libraries

Here are the required libraries for this program:

```
from random import randint
```

The program needs a random number generator to implement the artificial intelligence (AI) for the computer. The computer strategy is to randomly choose either rock, scissors, or paper.

Variables

Here are some initial variables for the program:

```
arr = ["rock","scissors","paper"]
compWins = 0
humanWins = 0
```

The `arr` variable is an array of strings. An array is an excellent choice to store the item names, because its indexes match the corresponding items (i.e., `"rock"` is at index `0`, `"scissors"` is at index `1`, and `"paper"` is at index `2`). The program will use this array to output the human and computer choices to the console. The `compWins` and `humanWins` variables count the number of wins by the human and computer players. When one of these variables reaches `3`, the game is over.

Welcome Messages

Two `print()` statements at the beginning of the program welcome the user to the game:

```
print("Welcome to Rock, Scissors, Paper!")
print("Win 3 out of 5 to win the game!")
```

Game Loop

A single While loop continues to play games until either the human or the computer earns 3 wins. Here is the main game loop

```
while (True):
    compChoice = randint(0,2)
    print('Enter rock(0), scissors(1), or paper(2).')
    humanChoice = int( input('Your choice: ') )

    if (humanChoice < 0 or humanChoice > 2):
        print("Invalid Entry. Try again.")
        continue

    print("You: " + arr[humanChoice] + ".")
    print("Computer: " + arr[compChoice] + ".")

    if (humanChoice == compChoice):
        print("Tie. Replaying...")
        print
        continue
    if ( (humanChoice == 0 and compChoice == 1) or
```

```
18            (humanChoice == 1 and compChoice == 2) or
19            (humanChoice == 2 and compChoice == 0) ):
20           print("You won!")
21           humanWins += 1
22       else:
23           print("Comnputer won!")
24           compWins += 1
25       print
26
27       if (humanWins == 3 or compWins == 3):
28           break
```

The condition on Line 1 will always be true, so it seems like the loop will execute forever. However, statements in the loop block will terminate the loop when either the human or computer gains three wins. Line 2 calls the `randint()` library function to return a random number from the range 0, 1, 2 and assign it to the `compChoice` variable. This is the simple AI random strategy. Line 3 prints an informative message to tell the user which number corresponds to which item. Line 4 prompts the user to input a choice, converts the value to an integer, and assigns the value to the `humanChoice` variable. The If-Then statement on Lines 6-8 checks if the `humanChoice` variable is invalid. If it is, Line 7 prints an error message, and Line 8 executes the `continue` statement to return to the top of the While loop to retry the game. If the program reaches Line 10, then the human choice is valid. Lines 10-11 print the human and computer choices. They use the `humanChoice` and `compChoice` variables as indexes into the `arr` array to retrieve the corresponding item name. Lines 13-16 check for the situation where the human and computer pick the same choice (i.e., a tie). If it is a tie, Line 14 prints a message, Line 15 prints a blank line, and Line 16 returns execution to the top of the loop for the next game. If it is *not* a tie, then execution continues on Line 17. The If-Then-Else statement on Lines 17-24 determine the winner for this round. If the compound condition on Lines 17-19 is `True`, then the human won the round. In this case, Line 20 prints a message, and Line 21 increases the `humanWins` variable by `1`. If the condition on Lines 17-19 is `False`, then the computer won the round. In this case, Line 23 prints a message, and Line 24 increases the `compWins` variable by `1`. Execution continues to Line 25 and the program prints a blank line. The If-Then statement on Line 27 checks if either the human or computer has 3 wins. If so, the game is over, and Line 28 executes the `break` statement to exit the While loop. If not, then execution returns to Line 1 for the next game.

Final Message

The last task of the program is to output the winner of the game. This If-Then-Else statement appears at the end of the program, after the While loop:

```
if (humanWins == 3):
    result = str(humanWins) + "-" + str(compWins)
    print("You won " + result + ".")
else:
    result =  str(compWins) + "-" + str(humanWins)
    print("Computer won " + result + ".")
```

The If-Then-Else statement outputs the winner and the score.

Source Code

Here is the complete source code for the Rock, Scissors, Paper program:

```
from random import randint

arr = ["rock","scissors","paper"]
compWins = 0
humanWins = 0

print("Welcome to Rock, Scissors, Paper!")
print("Win 3 out of 5 to win the game!")

while (True):
    compChoice = randint(0,2)
    print('Enter rock(0), scissors(1), or paper(2).')
    humanChoice = int( input('Your choice: ') )

    if (humanChoice < 0 or humanChoice > 2):
        print("Invalid Entry. Try again.")
        continue

    print("You: " + arr[humanChoice] + ".")
    print("Computer: " + arr[compChoice] + ".")

    if (humanChoice == compChoice):
        print("Tie. Replaying...")
```

```
        print
        continue
    if ( (humanChoice == 0 and compChoice == 1) or
         (humanChoice == 1 and compChoice == 2) or
         (humanChoice == 2 and compChoice == 0) ):
        print("You won!")
        humanWins += 1
    else:
        print("Comnputer won!")
        compWins += 1
    print

    if (humanWins == 3 or compWins == 3):
        break

if (humanWins == 3):
    result = str(humanWins) + "-" + str(compWins)
    print("You won " + result + ".")
else:
    result =  str(compWins) + "-" + str(humanWins)
    print("Computer won " + result + ".")
```

Here is a sample run for the program:

```
Welcome to Rock, Scissors, Paper!
Win 3 out of 5 to win the game!
Enter rock(0), scissors(1), or paper(2).
Your choice: 0
You: rock.
Computer: paper.
Comnputer won!

Enter rock(0), scissors(1), or paper(2).
Your choice: 1
You: scissors.
Computer: rock.
Comnputer won!

Enter rock(0), scissors(1), or paper(2).
Your choice: 2
You: paper.
```

```
Computer: rock.
You won!

Enter rock(0), scissors(1), or paper(2).
Your choice: 2
You: paper.
Computer: rock.
You won!

Enter rock(0), scissors(1), or paper(2).
Your choice: 1
You: scissors.
Computer: scissors.
Tie. Replaying...

Enter rock(0), scissors(1), or paper(2).
Your choice: 0
You: rock.
Computer: paper.
Comnputer won!

Computer won 3-2.
```

Discussion

The Rock, Scissors, Paper program is a fun game where a human plays against the computer. Once again, the task requires several programming concepts to implement the game. The program takes advantage of a built-in random number generator to implement the computer AI strategy. Beating the computer in this game takes a little luck.

Tic-Tac-Toe

Tic-Tac-Toe is a paper and pencil game for two players. There is a 3 x 3 grid. One player is 'X', and the other player is 'O'. The player who is 'X' goes first. Players take turns marking the grid with their letters. The first player who gets three letters in a row, column, or diagonal wins the game. Here is a sample Tic-Tac-Toe board after three turns:

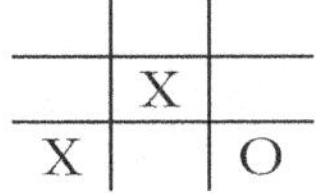

In this sample board, it is time for player 'O' to move. Player 'O' *must* mark the top right square to prevent player 'X' from winning with a diagonal.

The goal of this programming problem is to create a one player Tic-Tac-

Toe game, where a human player competes against an AI player. The program will play one game of Tic-Tac-Toe.

Assumptions

Here are the assumptions of the program:

1. This program assumes that the human ('X') moves first, and the computer ('O') moves second in *every* game.
2. If the human makes an invalid move, then the human loses that turn, and the computer makes the next move.
3. The '.' character represents an empty space on the board.

Libraries

Here are the required libraries for this program:

```
from random import randint
```

The program needs a random number generator to implement the artificial intelligence (AI) for the computer. The computer strategy is to randomly choose an open space on the Tic-Tac-Toe board.

Variables

Here is an initial variable to declare and initialize:

```
total_moves = 0
```

The `total_moves` variable counts the total number of moves made by either the human or the computer. If the count reaches `9`, then the game is over, since there are only 9 possible moves.

Board Representation

A good way to represent the Tic-Tac-Toe board is a two-dimensional list:

```
board = [
    ['.','.','.'],
    ['.','.','.'],
    ['.','.','.']
    ]
```

The two-dimensional list above represents a Tic-Tac-Toe board. It has three rows and three columns. Initially, each element is the empty space character ('.'), since the game has yet to begin. A two-dimensional list has two indexes. Since this is a 3 x 3 list, both indexes are in the range `0`, `1`, `2`. The first index is the row. The second index is the column. For example, the center square is at `board[1][1]` and the top right square is at `board[0][2]`.

There must be a way to print the board to the user. Here is a procedure to print the current board to the console:

```
1   def printBoard(b):
2       str = ""
3       for row in range(0, 3):
4           for col in range(0, 3):
5               str = str + b[row][col] + " "
6           str += "\n"
7       print(str)
```

Line 1 defines a procedure named **printBoard()** that takes one parameter **b**, which is the game board (i.e., two-dimensional list). Line 2 declares and initializes a variable **str** to store the current board as a string. The For loop on Lines 3-6 has a nested For loop. The outer For loop provides the index for each row. The inner For loop provides the index for each column. These two loops retrieve all elements of the board and add the elements to the **str** variable, with newline characters between each row. Line 7 is outside both loops. It prints the **str** variable to the console. Here is a sample output of this procedure, given some sample **board**:

```
X O O
O X O
O O X
```

Check for a Winner

The program must check the board for a row, column, or diagonal winner. A straightforward way to check for a winner is to check if all the elements are equal, but not equal to the empty space character ('.'). The program must check all rows, columns, and diagonals in this manner, until it finds a winner (if any). Here is a function that checks for a winner on the board:

```
def isWinner(b):

    # check for row winner
    for row in range(0, 3):
        if (b[row][0] == b[row][1] and
            b[row][0] == b[row][2] and
            b[row][0] != '.'):
            return b[row][0]
```

```
9
10      # check for column winner
11      for col in range(0, 3):
12          if (b[0][col] == b[1][col] and
13              b[0][col] == b[2][col] and
14              b[0][col] != '.'):
15              return b[0][col]
16
17      # check one diagonal winner
18      if (b[0][0] == b[1][1] and
19          b[0][0] == b[2][2] and
20          b[0][0] != '.'):
21          return b[0][0]
22
23      # check other diagonal winner
24      if (b[2][0] == b[1][1] and
25          b[2][0] == b[0][2] and
26          b[2][0] != '.'):
27          return b[2][0]
28
29      # no winner yet
30      return '.'
```

Line 1 declares a function named `isWinner()`. The function takes one parameter `b`, which is the game board. Lines 4-8 of this function loop through all the rows to check for a row winner. If there is a winner, the function immediately returns the winning letter (either 'X' or 'O') on Line 8. If there is no row winner, the function continues to Line 11. In a similar manner, Lines 11-15 check for a column winner. If there is no column winner, the function continues to Line 18. Lines 18-21 check one diagonal for a winner. Lines 24-27 check the other diagonal for a winner. If there are no diagonal winners, the function proceeds to Line 30 and returns the empty space character (`'.'`) to indicate that there are no winners on the current board. The program will call the `isWinner()` function after each turn, to check for a winner.

Computer Move

The program must decide where the computer will move on the board. A simple AI for this game is to randomly select the first available space on the board. Here is a procedure to do just that:

```
1   def getComputerMove(b):
2       global total_moves
3       if (total_moves >= 9):
4           return # no more moves, just return
5
6       row = 0;
7       col = 0;
8       while(True):
9           row = randint(0,2)
10          col = randint(0,2)
11          if (b[row][col] == '.'):
12              break
13
14      b[row][col] = 'O'
15      total_moves += 1
```

Line 1 declares a procedure named **getComputerMove()**. The procedure takes one parameter **b**, which is the game board. Line 2 of the program indicates that the **total_moves** variable is declared globally, outside the procedure. Lines 3-4 check to see if there are no more moves. If so, the procedure returns immediately. Otherwise, execution continues to Line 6. Lines 6-7 declare and initialize variables for the row and column indexes. The While loop on Lines 8-12 keep looping until the program finds an empty space in the board. Line 9 calls the **randint()** function to return a random integer from the range **0**, **1**, **2**. This will be the potential row index. Line 10 performs similar logic to retrieve the potential column index. Line 11 checks to see if the space at that row and column is empty (**'.'**). If it is, then there is an open space on the board, and the program executes the **break** statement on Line 12 to exit the loop. Otherwise, the While loop executes again. When the program reaches Line 14, the column and row indexes are the coordinates of an empty space on the board. Line 14 executes to make the computer move on the board. Line 15 increases the **total_moves** variable by **1**.

Human Move

To implement the human move, the program must display the current board and ask the human to make a move. The human must supply the row (**0**, **1**, or **2**) and the column (**0**, **1**, or **2**) of the space to move to. Here is a procedure to get the human move:

```
def getHumanMove(b):
```

```
2       global total_moves
3       if (total_moves >= 9):
4           return # no more moves, just return
5
6       printBoard(b)
7
8       row = int( input('Enter row(0,1,2): ') )
9       col = int( input('Enter col(0,1,2): ') )
10
11      if (row < 0 or row > 2):
12          return
13
14      if (col < 0 or col > 2):
15          return
16
17      if (b[row][col] != '.'):
18          return
19
20      b[row][col] = 'X'
21      total_moves += 1
```

Line 1 declares a procedure named `getHumanMove()`. The procedure takes one parameter `b`, which is the game board. Line 2 of the program indicates that the `total_moves` variable is declared globally, outside the procedure. Lines 3-4 check to see if there are no more moves. If so, the procedure returns immediately. Otherwise, execution continues to Line 6. Line 6 calls the `printBoard()` procedure to print the current board, so the user can decide where to move. This is an example of a procedure calling another procedure. Lines 8-9 ask the user to input a row and column, and they convert the values to integers. Lines 11-15 make sure that the row and column values are valid indexes for this board. If not, the human loses a turn, and the procedure returns immediately. Lines17-18 check to see if the space is empty. If not, the human loses a turn, and the procedure returns immediately. If the procedure reaches Line 20, that means it is a valid move, and the program marks the space with an `'X'`. Line 21 increases the `total_moves` variable by `1`.

Main Logic

The main logic of the program can now take advantage of the procedures and functions defined above. The logic is compact and straightforward:

```
1   foundWinner = False
2   while (total_moves < 9):
3       getHumanMove(board)
4       getComputerMove(board)
5       winner = isWinner(board)
6       if (winner != '.'):
7           printBoard(board)
8           print(winner + " wins!")
9           foundWinner = True
10          break
11
12  if (not foundWinner):
13      printBoard(board)
14      print("Tie game.")
```

Line 1 declares a variable named `foundWinner` and initializes it to `False`. The While loop on Line 2 continues until either the `total_moves` variable reaches `9` or the program declares a winner. Line 3 calls the `getHumanMove()` procedure, passing it the `board` variable. Line 4 calls the `getComputerMove()` procedure, passing it the `board` variable. Line 5 calls the `isWinner()` function to retrieve the winner (if any). If the condition on Line 6 is `True`, the program prints the board, prints the winner, sets the `foundWinner` variable to `True`, and breaks out of the While loop. The If-Then statement on Lines 12-14 handle the case where the game ends in a tie.

Source Code

Here is the complete source code for the Tic, Tac, Toe program:

```
from random import randint

total_moves = 0

board = [
    ['.','.','.'],
    ['.','.','.'],
    ['.','.','.']
    ]

def printBoard(b):
```

```
    str = ""
    for row in range(0, 3):
        for col in range(0, 3):
            str = str + b[row][col] + " "
        str += "\n"
    print(str)

def isWinner(b):

    # check for row winner
    for row in range(0, 3):
        if (b[row][0] == b[row][1] and
            b[row][0] == b[row][2] and
            b[row][0] != '.'):
            return b[row][0]

    # check for column winner
    for col in range(0, 3):
        if (b[0][col] == b[1][col] and
            b[0][col] == b[2][col] and
            b[0][col] != '.'):
            return b[0][col]

    # check one diagonal winner
    if (b[0][0] == b[1][1] and
        b[0][0] == b[2][2] and
        b[0][0] != '.'):
        return b[0][0]

    # check other diagonal winner
    if (b[2][0] == b[1][1] and
        b[2][0] == b[0][2] and
        b[2][0] != '.'):
        return b[2][0]

    # no winner yet
    return '.'
```

```

def getComputerMove(b):
    global total_moves
    if (total_moves >= 9):
        return # no more moves, just return

    row = 0;
    col = 0;
    while(True):
        row = randint(0,2)
        col = randint(0,2)
        if (b[row][col] == '.'):
            break

    b[row][col] = 'O'
    total_moves += 1

def getHumanMove(b):
    global total_moves
    if (total_moves >= 9):
        return # no more moves, just return

    printBoard(b)

    row = int( input('Enter row(0,1,2): ') )
    col = int( input('Enter col(0,1,2): ') )

    if (row < 0 or row > 2):
        return

    if (col < 0 or col > 2):
        return

    if (b[row][col] != '.'):
        return

    b[row][col] = 'X'
```

```
    total_moves += 1

# main program
foundWinner = False
while (total_moves < 9):
    getHumanMove(board)
    getComputerMove(board)
    winner = isWinner(board)
    if (winner != '.'):
        printBoard(board)
        print(winner + " wins!")
        foundWinner = True
        break

if (not foundWinner):
    printBoard(board)
    print("Tie game.")
```

Here is a sample run for the program:

```
. . .
. . .
. . .

Enter row(0,1,2): 0
Enter col(0,1,2): 0
X . .
. O .
. . .

Enter row(0,1,2): 1
Enter col(0,1,2): 2
X . .
. O X
. . O

Enter row(0,1,2): 1
Enter col(0,1,2): 0
X . O
X O X
. . O
```

```
Enter row(0,1,2): 2
Enter col(0,1,2): 0
X . O
X O X
X O O

X wins!
```

Discussion

The Tic-Tac-Toe program uses many of the programming concepts discussed in this book. The program creates several modules to simplify and organize the overall task. This makes the final While loop in the main part of the program simple and easy to understand.

Fizz Buzz

Fizz Buzz is a popular interview question for prospective programmers. The task is simple:

1. Loop through the numbers 1 to 100.
2. If the number is divisible by 3, print "Fizz".
3. If the number is divisible by 5, print "Buzz".
4. If the number is divisible by both 3 and 5, print "FizzBuzz".
5. Otherwise, just print the number itself.

Here is a shortened version of the output:

```
1
2
Fizz
4
Buzz
Fizz
7
8
Fizz
Buzz
11
Fizz
13
14
FizzBuzz
16
.
```

```
.
.
Fizz
94
Buzz
Fizz
97
98
Fizz
Buzz
```

How would you approach this program? What programming concepts would you use? Think about it for a minute before continuing to the next section.

The Ugly Way

A straightforward, but ugly way to complete this task is a program like this:

```
 1  print("1")
 2  print("2")
 3  print("Fizz")
 4  print("4")
 5  print("Buzz")
 6  .
 7  .
 8  .
 9  print("97")
10  print("98")
11  print("Fizz")
12  print("Buzz")
```

In this program, Lines 6-8 represent the lines that have been omitted for conciseness. Although this program is technically correct, no employer will hire you for such a brute force attempt. Imagine if the task was to loop through the range 1 to 1,000,000. That would be a very tedious program to write using this ugly approach. There are better ways to solve this problem.

An Elegant Way

A more elegant way to solve this problem is to use a loop. But first, declare a variable `s` to hold the entire output of the program:

```
s = ""
```

Since the program must loop through the numbers `1` to `100`, then the following For loop is a good start:

```
for num in range(1, 101):
```

This For loop loops through the values `1` to `100` (inclusive) and uses an index variable named `num`. Inside the For loop, determine if the current number (in the `num` variable) is divisible by 3 and divisible by 5. Use two Boolean variables to hold those results:

```
1       div3 = (num % 3 == 0)
2       div5 = (num % 5 == 0)
```

The `div3` variable on Line 1 is a Boolean variable that indicates if `num` is divisible by `3`. Line 1 uses the modulus (`%`) operator with the `num` variable to calculate the remainder when dividing `num` by `3`. If the remainder is `0`, then the condition inside the parentheses is `True`, and the program assigns `True` to the `div3` variable. Line 2 performs similar logic to determine if `num` is divisible by `5`.

Now that the program knows if `num` is divisible by `3` or `5`, it may begin building the output string. If `num` is not divisible by `3` or `5`, then the program must put the number itself in the output string:

```
1       if (not div3 and not div5):
2           s = s + str(num) + '\n'
3           continue
```

Line 1 is an If-Then statement that checks for this case. Line 2 adds a string version of the `num` variable to the output string `s`, followed by a newline character. Line 3 executes the continue statement to immediately return to the top of the loop to get the next value of the `num` variable.

If the condition on Line 1 of the previous program is `False`, that means that the program will print either "Fizz", "Buzz", or "FizzBuzz". This If-Then statement checks if "Fizz" should be added to the output string:

```
    if (num % 3 == 0):
        s = s + "Fizz"
```

This If-Then statement checks if "Buzz" should be added to the output string:

```
    if (num % 5 == 0):
        s = s + "Buzz"
```

Note that if `num` is divisible by both `3` and `5`, "FizzBuzz" will appear in the output string. The last line of the For loop is to add a newline character to the output string `s`:

```
    s = s + '\n'
```

The last line of the program, after the For loop, prints the output string `s`:

```
print(s)
```

Here is the complete source code listing of the FizzBuzz solution:

```
s = ""
for num in range(1, 101):
    div3 = (num % 3 == 0)
    div5 = (num % 5 == 0)
    if (not div3 and not div5):
        s = s + str(num) + '\n'
        continue
    if (num % 3 == 0):
        s = s + "Fizz"
    if (num % 5 == 0):
        s = s + "Buzz"
    s = s + '\n'
print(s)
```

Discussion

There are many possible solutions to the FizzBuzz problem. The more elegant solutions incorporate a loop and selection statements. Although the previous example is short, devising this solution requires thought. The first step is to understand the basic programming concepts. Then you can figure out how to use them to solve any programming task.

Summary

The case studies in this chapter show how to use and combine the basic programming concepts in this book. Each program you write increases your understanding of the basic programming concepts. Soon you will be able to easily and effortlessly apply these programming concepts to solve big programming problems. Keep practicing by writing lots of programs. This is the best way to increase your programming skills. *Experience is the best teacher.* Good luck to you and enjoy programming!

12 FINAL THOUGHTS

This book takes a super simple approach to programming. It teaches the basic programming concepts that most languages have. The examples in this book are short and simple. They explain programming concepts in a straightforward way. Learning the basic programming concepts is important, because it makes it easy to learn other programming languages.

The Python programming language is an excellent choice for this book. It is easy to use, free, and widely available. Python is very popular in the industry today.

This book omits some programming details and concepts. This is by design. It can be overwhelming to try to learn everything about programming all at once. The reality is that you don't even need all the programming details to become a programmer. A program only needs the subset of programming concepts that implements the task at hand. You can learn the other programming details when you need to.

Finally, continue your programming journey on your own. Now that you know the basic programming concepts, you can write your own programs. Practice a lot. Write a program a day, no matter how small. Read about programming. This self-study is extremely valuable. It will give you valuable experience. You now have the knowledge to practice programming. If you do that, you will become an expert soon.

Good luck and enjoy programming!

- Ed

ABOUT THE AUTHOR

I am a full-time software engineer at The MITRE Corporation. I am also a part-time computer science professor at Monmouth University and Brookdale Community College. I enjoy teaching students. If a student is on the fence about pursuing computer science, I do my best to convert them! I realize that teaching helps me in many ways. Time flies when I am in the classroom.

I have a Doctor of Engineering from George Washington University, a Master of Science in Computer Science from New Jersey Institute of Technology, and a Bachelor of Arts in Computer Science from Rutgers College. That is enough. I am done with school.

I am reachable by email, edwintorres@gwu.edu.

Thanks for reading!

The author's affiliation with The MITRE Corporation is provided for identification purposes only, and is not intended to convey or imply MITRE's concurrence with, or support for, the positions, opinions or viewpoints expressed by the author.

Made in the USA
Middletown, DE
02 March 2020

85690540R00066